Homer's ILIAD

DAVID SIDER
DEPARTMENT OF CLASSICS
BROOKLYN COLLEGE

and

DAVID KONSTAN
COLUMBIA UNIVERSITY

Edited by

STANLEY BRODWIN
ASSISTANT PROFESSOR
HOFSTRA UNIVERSITY

MONARCH PRESS

Copyright © 1963, 1964, 1966 by
SIMON & SCHUSTER, Inc.

All rights reserved including the right of reproduction in whole or in part in any form.

Published by
MONARCH PRESS
A Simon & Schuster division of
Gulf & Western Corporation
Simon & Schuster Building
1230 Avenue of the Americas
New York, N.Y. 10020

Manufactured in the United States of America

Printed and Bound by Semline, Inc.

1 2 3 4 5 6 7 8 9 10

ISBN: 0-671-00501-4

Library of Congress Catalog Card Number: 65-7187

CONTENTS

one   **THE HISTORY**   **5**

     The Greek and Trojan War; archeological and historical confirmation   5

     The poetic traditions of Homer's Greece; the epic cycle   10

two   **THE BOOK: THE ILIAD**   **18**

     Mythical structure and ideals of *The Iliad*   18

     Detailed summary with analytic comment

Book I:	The Plague and the Wrath	23
Book II:	The Dream. The Catalogue of Ships	30
Book III:	Oaths. The Battle of Alexander and Menelaus	33
Book IV:	The Breaking of the Oaths	37
Book V:	The Aristeia of Diomedes	40
Book VI:	Hector and Andromache	44
Book VII:	The Battle between Hector and Aias	48
Book VIII:	The Short Battle	51
Book IX:	The Embassy to Achilles	55
Book X:	The Doloneia	61
Book XI:	The Aristeia of Agamemnon	63
Book XII:	The Battle by the Wall	66
Book XIII:	The Battle by the Ships	68
Book XIV:	The Deceiving of Zeus	71
Book XV:	The Retreat from the Ships	75
Book XVI:	The Patrocleia	79
Book XVII:	The Aristeia of Menelaus	83
Book XVIII:	The Shield of Achilles	86
Book XIX:	The Preparation for Battle	91
Book XX:	The Battle of the Gods	94
Book XXI:	The Battle by the River	98
Book XXII:	The Death of Hector	102
Book XXIII:	The Funeral Games	107
Book XXIV:	The Ransoming of Hector	112

three	THE CHARACTERS	**118**
	Description and analysis of the characters and deities	
four	COMMENTARY	**127**
	An historical survey of the controversies over Homer and *The Iliad* 127	
	Analytic commentary on the techniques, motifs, digressions, and themes in *The Iliad* 129	
five	TEST QUESTIONS	**135**
	Essay questions and detailed answers	
six	FURTHER READING	**142**
	A bibliography for the book and the author	

INTRODUCTION

In order to appreciate the *Iliad* more fully, it is necessary to know as much as possible of the background of the work. We must try, to the best of our ability, to put ourselves in the place of Homer's audience. This introduction will give a summary of the material needed for a proper understanding of the *Iliad*. Consult the bibliography at the end of the book for a list of books that present this background material in greater detail.

GREECE & THE TROJAN WAR. There are two epics that Homer is said to have written: the *Iliad* and the *Odyssey*. The story of the *Iliad* unfolds toward the end of the Trojan War—a war between the Greeks and the Trojans. The *Odyssey* is the story of the return of one of the Greek generals who fought in the Trojan War. All readers of the *Odyssey* are expected to know the story of the *Iliad* and the Trojan War.

Is there any truth to the tale of this war? Or is it merely a story that gained great popularity in Greece, though it has no historical basis? The Greeks after Homer believed in his geography, even to the point of assigning actual locations to places that are a part of Homer's fairy land. But for many years during the modern era, people thought that there had never been a Trojan War. Some people thought that there had never even been a city named Troy.

THE BIRTH OF ARCHEOLOGY. There was one person, however, who did believe in Troy. Heinrich Schliemann had read Homer as a boy and had gained a great enthusiasm for the *Iliad* and the *Odyssey*—an enthusiasm that stayed with him for the rest of his life. In 1870 he started digging at the town at Hissarlik, in Turkey, where he believed Troy was buried. His discovery, which confirmed his belief, surprised everyone and forced scholars to admit the existence of this fabled city. He also uncovered Pylos, Nestor's city, and Mycenae, the city ruled by Agamemnon, the leader of the Greek forces in the *Iliad*.

Heinrich Schliemann's discovery made people realize the value of archeology. Since his first, and in many ways, crude excavations, archeologists have dug up other Greek cities of the time of the Trojan War, and have returned to Troy to study in greater detail the city that Homer described more than twenty-five hundred years ago. Archeologists can now tell us where many of Homer's cities were. And from the excavations of these cities they have found many of the objects described by Homer—mixing bowls, armor, bows, etc. Their research also clarifies the details of the Homeric house, which is difficult to reconstruct on the basis of Homer alone. But their research also raises problems, for this new archeological evidence shows that Homer was describing no particular period of history. Thus, a warrior in the *Iliad* might ride into battle on a chariot of the ninth century B.C.; he might fight in a battle formation of the eighth century, holding a spear of the twelfth century. This disregard of historical accuracy has been used as evidence by some scholars to demonstrate that more than one person composed each of the epics. This problem will be considered in the section of the Critical Commentary dealing with the "Homeric Question."

EGYPTIAN AND HITTITE EVIDENCE. The value of archeology in studying Homer can be more fully appreciated when it is realized that, until quite recently, archeology provided the only source of evidence contemporary with the events of the poem, aside from a few Egyptian documents that mentioned the Greeks. Then in the 1920's Hittite, the language of an Indo-European people inhabiting Asia Minor, was deciphered. Records of this language, which are preserved on clay tablets, mention in several places a land called *Ahhiyawa*. Several scholars have identified this name with Achaea, a part of Greece (Homer frequently refers to the Greeks as Achaeans). The Ahhiyawans were, according to the Hittite tablets, a powerful race who had a large fleet of ships, as had the Achaeans. We know that the Hittites had a treaty with the Ahhiyawans, but the location of the land from which these allies came is nowhere mentioned in the tablets. Many scholars, therefore, still have doubts about equating the Ahhiyawans with the Achaeans despite the many other names on the tablets that are similar to Greek names, for example, Hittite Lukka and Greek Lycia, a town on the coast of Asia Minor that could have been known to the Hittites.

Some of these similarities are too strong and too frequent to be denied. For instance, a list of names on one of the Hittite tablets has on it the name Taruisha, which is followed by the name Uilusha. These names are very similar to Troy and Ilios, which is used by Homer as another name for Troy. Furthermore, from another tablet we know that at one time the king of Uilusha was named Alaksandus, a name very similar to Alexander (Paris of the *Iliad* is also called Alexander).

LINEAR B. Another language that was recently (1953) deciphered and that sheds light on the time of the Trojan War is Linear B. Michael Ventris, after working for many years, succeeded

in proving that Linear B is actually Greek, but written in a strange
alphabet. The decipherment of Linear B (so called to distinguish it
from Linear A, a language written in the same alphabet, but not yet
deciphered) made scholars re-examine the importance of Greek
domination from 1500-1150 B.C. over the Greek mainland and the
Aegean Sea, a domination earlier scholars had underestimated.

THE FIRST GREEKS Thus, from these contemporary sources,
as well as from the *Iliad* and the *Odyssey*, a fairly complete picture
of life during the Mycenaean period can be obtained. The Greeks
of this time were the descendants of the original Greek colonists
who entered the Greek mainland about 2000 B.C. and merged with
the original inhabitants of this land. They brought with them horses,
wheel-made pottery, the idea of fortified towns and, of course, the
Greek language.

By the middle of the sixteenth century B.C. the most powerful
Greek city was Mycenae. Through foreign trade, mostly with Egypt,
Mycenae was able to gain great wealth and power. Its citizens conquered Crete, the strongest outpost of the pre-Greek people of the
Aegean. For 400 years (1550-1150 B.C.) Mycenae ruled the
Aegean, founding many colonies as its trade expanded. Many of
these colonies in later classical times, became famous on their own,
for example, Miletus and Rhodes. Mycenae attacked Thebes. Part
of this story is told in *The Seven Against Thebes*, a play by Aeschylus, a Greek dramatist of the sixth century B.C. Mycenaens were
powerful enough to attack Egypt twice—in 1225 and again in 1195.
Their assault on Troy is the Trojan War of Greek myth. This period
of Mycenaean power ended about 1150 with the Dorian invasion.
The Dorians, the last race of Greeks to overrun the mainland,
brought about the downfall of Mycenaean civilization, starting
what is known as the Dark Ages of Greece (1150-900).

ECONOMY DURING MYCENAEN TIMES. During the period
of the Trojan War, Greece was broken up into many small kingdoms, living under a social and economic system similar to that of
the Middle Ages in Europe. The main economic unit was the *oikos*,
the equivalent to the manor of the later feudal system. Surrounding
the *oikos* was enough farm and pasture land to support the *oikos*-
owner, his family, and his servants and slaves. The servants had
various functions to perform, such as herding the pigs, goats, and
cattle kept by all *oikoi* (the plural of *oikos*). They also had duties
to perform in the house. Since the main source of slaves was
through warfare, most of the slaves in any household were women,
for it was the practice among victorious Greeks to kill all the men
they conquered. These female slaves helped the mistress of the
house in weaving, washing and nursing.

Few of the servants and slaves had specialized skills. The minstrels, carpenters, metal-workers, doctors and prophets formed a class by themselves. They were not attached to any one house, but went wherever their services were called for. Thus, each *oikos* was nearly a self-sufficient unit, independent of every other household, although the *oikos*-owner did owe allegiance to the king of his land. Thus, the householders and their families formed an aristocracy. All other people, whatever their position, were part of the masses.

It was only during a war that the household-owners acted together. The wars in which they were engaged were probably not fought for the acquisition of land, but rather to gain metals: gold, silver, copper, iron. Some scholars think that the historical Trojan War was actually a raid to obtain iron. The Greeks themselves saw no difference between a war and a private raid. Odysseus and his men, for example, in Book IX of the *Odyssey*, saw nothing wrong with interrupting their journey home to sack the city of Ismaros, taking all the booty and wives they could carry.

ASSEMBLIES. During peacetime the only official place for the nobles to meet was at the assembly, which was called by the king. These assemblies were called whenever the king had an important decision to make concerning all the nobles (that is, all the *oikos*-owners) in his land. Although he had the power to make decisions without consulting them, he rarely did so. At an assembly the nobles would discuss the problem before them, judging it on the basis of their local traditions. It is no wonder that Homer considered the assembly a vital part of any civilized society. For example, when in the *Odyssey* he describes the barbaric Cyclopes (Book IX), Homer is quick to point out that they have no assemblies, but live without traditions. On the other hand, the Phaeacians (*Od.* Books VI, VII, VIII), whom Homer considers to be overly civilized, are constantly having assemblies. On the battlefield, far from home, Agamemnon in the *Iliad* carries on this custom by continuing to hold assemblies to discuss matters of importance to the Greek warriors.

GUESTS AND HOSTS. In a world in which contact among nobles living in the same country was limited to these infrequent assemblies, contact among nobles living in different lands was even more irregular. There was no king and no law to regulate such "international" affairs. Instead, people had to depend on each other's good faith. From this dependence an elaborate tradition developed concerning the relationship between travellers and their hosts. For example, hosts were expected to protect their guests from harm. Of course the guest had responsibilities to his host. The traditional cause of the Trojan War is a breach of faith on the part of a guest. Paris (also called Alexander), who was a guest in the house of Menelaus, King of Sparta, seduced Menelaus' wife Helen and ran away with her to his native city, Troy. Menelaus and his brother led an army of Greeks to Troy in order to destroy the city for harboring such a great sinner as Paris. The importance in the Greek mind of the guest-host relationship can be seen in the fact that Zeus, the mightiest of the gods, was considered to be the guardian of these relations.

TROJAN ARCHEOLOGY. Let us now return to the subject of Troy. Schliemann, the first to excavate the site, recognized that there had been more than one city built at that location. In fact, nine levels, indicating nine towns, were noted. It remained for later archeologists to make further refinements in the number of levels and to decide which of the levels was the Troy of the Trojan War.

Since any fortress built on this site could control all shipping traffic through the Dardanelles, the waterway leading from the Aegean Sea to the Euxine Sea, the site has been occupied almost continuously from 3200 B.C. until the present time. The first settlement was originally quite small (in the Early Bronze Age). Later it increased its fortifications and finally was completely destroyed by fire.

The second level, Troy II, as it is designated by archeologists, was built upon the ruins of Troy II immediately after the fire. It too expanded as it grew more prosperous, and it too was destroyed by fire. Troy II was followed, logically enough, by Troys III, IV and V. Each of these levels lasted about a hundred years and was inhabited by the same race of people.

TROY VI. The next level, built about the year 1900 B.C., was inhabited by a new people. This fact can be demonstrated by the remains of their buildings and of their pottery, which differ in many ways from those of the previous levels. What is most interesting about these new Trojans is that they seem to have been closely related to the Greeks. They were probably part of the same movement that had started in Central Europe and had spread out in all directions, extending finally as far as Ireland and India (hence the name Indo-European for all the languages descended from this original group). One piece of evidence for this close relationship between the Greeks and the Trojans is the pottery remains found in Troy VI. This pottery was made with a certain technique that was used elsewhere only by the Greeks of Mycenae. The possibility that these pots were imported from Mycenae (which at this time was carrying on its trading activities throughout the Aegean area) was rejected because it is only the technique of manufacture that is the same, not the styles. This technique is sufficiently complicated to rule out the possibility that the people of Mycenae and Troy developed it independently of one another. The only possibility remaining is that both groups learned it from the same source, their ancestors, and that these ancestors, hence, were the same people for both Troy and Greece. In addition to this pottery technique (Minyan pottery), another link between Troy and Greece is the horse. The Greeks were the first to bring the horse to the Greek mainland, and there are no traces of horses in Troy before Troy VI.

"TROY." Troy VI was destroyed by an earthquake in the year 1275. The next level, designated as Troy VIIa by archeologists, was built soon after the destruction of Troy VI by the same people. There are several facts about the remains of this level which are of great interest to us. First, all of the houses had huge storage jars, as if they needed to maintain a lot of food while they were being besieged; second, the town was destroyed by fire, the usual fate of a conquered city; third, two skeletons were found lying out in the open with the appearance of having been killed by a weapon; fourth, Troy VIIa was inhabited during the time that ancient Greek historians, working without the aid of archeology, said the Trojan War was fought. The probable date for the destruction of Troy VIIa is 1250, the very date given for the Trojan War by Herodotus, a Greek historian of the fifth century B.C. It is certain, therefore, that if there ever was a Trojan War, this is where and when it was fought.

GREECE AFTER THE TROJAN WAR. From the preceding section it is easy to see that scholars have a great deal to say about the social and historical background of the *Iliad* and the *Odyssey*. But if we ask about Greece during the 400 years following the Trojan War, we are on less sure ground. The Trojan War was fought about a century before the influx of Dorian Greeks to the mainland. These Dorians spread out over western Greece, bringing about the end of the system of government described in the first section of this introduction. The Dorian invasion also meant that Greece was now without an alphabet, for the knowledge of writing Linear B was lost with the destruction of the major towns by the Dorians. For a period of about 400 years (1150-750 B.C.) until writing was reintroduced, there was no body of written literature in Greece. But this is not to say that there was no literature being composed, for poems were composed to be recited orally.

COMMUNITY SPIRIT IN MAINLAND GREECE. The type of poem that was composed depended on the society in which it was produced. The Dorians were a communal people. That is, they lived and worked together with very little conflict among individuals.

THE ILIAD

It was this community spirit which produced the Spartans, the foremost of the Dorians in the fifth and fourth centuries B.C. The poetry that developed from such a society—choral songs—aptly reflected the communal feelings of its inhabitants. These poems were not only sung by groups of people, but frequently exalted the very group spirit that gave rise to choral songs.

INDIVIDUALITY IN IONIA. In the eastern part of the Greek-speaking world and on the coast of Asia Minor, as well as on the islands of the Aegean, were the Ionian Greeks. Many of these Ionians were living in towns founded by Mycenae and by other towns during the period of expansion and trade. Here trade was still carried on with Egypt and other lands, although not to the extent that it was in the period of Mycenaean supremacy.

Instead of the community spirit that evolved in the west, a sense of individuality was maintained throughout Ionia (as the Aegean islands and the coast of Asia Minor are called). Quite naturally, the poetry of Ionia reflected this individuality. Instead of poems sung by many people, as among the Dorians, in Ionia the poems were recited by one person, and, what is more important, instead of poems about the community spirit, these were poems that exalted the spirit of the individual. The two long poems we have from this period, the *Iliad* and the *Odyssey,* praise individual accomplishments.

THE EPIC. One of the first questions to arise concerning the *Iliad* and the *Odyssey* is how, since there was no writing, anyone could memorize a poem the length of either of these two epics (about 350 pages in most books). It has been found to be generally true that in societies where there is no writing people's memories are better than those of people living in literate societies. Even today there are poets living in Yugoslavia capable of reciting, from memory, poems the length of the *Iliad*.

But a good memory is not the complete answer, for the minstrel, the bard who recited the poem, was expected to compose his own story, even though it might be based on traditional tales, such as those revolving about the Trojan War. A precise understanding of how a bard was able to compose and recite his poems was not to be had until recently. Before we can learn the answer to this question, however, we must first learn precisely what a Greek epic is.

EPIC METER. *An epic is a long poem, each line of which is in the same meter.* The meter of the *Iliad* and the *Odyssey* (and, because of their great influence, most subsequent epics) is dactylic hexameter. "Dactylic" means that the basic unit of each line is in the form $-\cup\cup$, where $--$ represents a metrically long syllable, $\cup$ a short syllable. It is called dactylic because it is like your finger, one long joint followed by two short ones—"dactylic" is Greek for "fingerlike." "Hexameter" tells us that six of these dactyls make up a line. In practice, one or more of the dactyls ($-\cup\cup$) might be replaced by a spondee ($--$), and the last foot is always a spondee. The line of the epic may be represented thus:

$$-\underline{\cup\cup} \mid -\underline{\cup\cup} \mid -\underline{\cup\cup} \mid -\underline{\cup\cup} \mid -\underline{\cup\cup} \mid --$$

Some lines may be all dactyls (except of course the last foot), for example the tenth line of Book I of the *Iliad*:

noúson aná straton órse kakén, olekónto de láoi,
$-\cup\cup \mid -\cup\cup \mid -\cup\cup \mid -\cup\cup \mid -\cup\cup \mid --$

Some may have many spondees, for example line 1 of Book XI of the *Iliad*:

Éos d'ék lecheón par' agaúou Títhonoío,
$-- \mid -\cup\cup \mid -\cup\cup \mid -- \mid -- \mid --$

In practice, the poet seems to have thought not in terms of feet (dactyls and spondees), but in terms of metrical limbs, or *cola*. That is, he thought of the line as a unit containing four, less often three such units, each containing a separate thought. A full discussion of this aspect of epic poetry would go beyond the scope of this introduction; see the article by Howard Porter listed in the bibliography.

Of course not all words can fit into this metrical scheme. For example, the combination   has no place in a dactylic line. Being barred from using certain words, the poet had to keep in mind, as he recited, a metrically proper word for each concept he might be called upon to use. But even a word that fits the dactylic meter cannot be placed anywhere in the line, but only where it fits. The poet had to remember not only the proper word but also the positions in the line where it could fit. Poets, hence, tended to remember whole phrases and, later, whole lines to express an oft-repeated thought. For example the frequently recurring phrase "when early-rising, rosy-fingered dawn appeared" is, in Greek, one line of dactylic hexameter.

ORAL TRADITION AND THE FORMULA. These useful words, phrases and lines were passed down from poet to poet until, by Homer's time (800-750 B.C.) it was possible to compose a long epic of great complexity and originality that was made up largely of formulas (as these standard words, phrases, and lines are called). It is thought that some of these formulas date back to the Trojan War itself, yet were kept by generations of poets, even though the

THE ILIAD

meanings of some of the words were lost, perhaps even to Homer. For example, Hermes is frequently called "argeiphontes." Some people translate the word as "the slayer of Argos," others as "brightly appearing." Over a period of centuries more and more phrases were originated and retained in the collective memory of the minstrels, thus increasing the store of formulas.

By Homer's time, every common word appeared in a number of formulas. The Greek word for ship, for example, appears in several phrases: balanced ship (2 feet), dark-prowed ship (3¼ feet) and curved ship (2½ feet). These three formulas fit at the end of the line. Thus, as the singer recites the first part of the line, he plans ahead to have 2, 2½, or 3¼ feet left at the end of the line, so that he may fit in one of the "ship" formulas.

HOW INDIVIDUAL POETS COMPOSED. In the case of a relatively common word like "ship" the poet rarely cares whether he calls the ship balanced, dark-prowed, or curved. Unfortunately, many people make the serious mistake of assuming that this is always so—that the poet does not care what formula he uses, so long as it fills out the line. These people have been especially critical of Homer's method of applying adjectives to names (epithets). In other words, what they are telling us is this: "As you read the *Iliad* and search for its meaning, ignore the epithets, for they do not mean anything. Homer put in these metrically convenient adjectives, because they fill out the line."

As an exmple of their thinking, let us use the name of Odysseus, one of the Greek generals fighting in Troy. If Homer wants to end the line with the name Odysseus he has several adjectives to go with the name. Thus, if he has two feet left ($-\cup\cup\,|\,--$), he will write *dios Odysseus* (divine Odysseus); if he has 2½ feet left ($\cup\cup\,|-\cup\cup\,|\,--$), he will write *polymetis Odysseus* (wily Odysseus); if he has 3¼ feet left ($\cup\,|-\cup\cup\,|-\cup\cup\,|--$), he will write *polytlas dios Odysseus* (much-suffering, divine Odysseus).

The people who maintain that these epithets have no meaning are led astray by the way that they phrase the problem. It is true that, given a set number of feet at the end of the line and a name to go with this number, there is usually only one adjective appropriate to the name to fill out the line. Therefore, they conclude, these adjectives are chosen solely for metrical convenience.

The conclusion would be true if their hypothesis were true—but it is not. The poet is not "given" a set number of feet to fill up with a name and an adjective. He controls the first half of the line as much as the last half. He decides whether there will be 2, 2½, 3¼, or any other number of feet left, and therefore he can decide in advance exactly which epithet he will use.

THE TEXT OF HOMER. Homer, the author of the *Iliad* and the *Odyssey*, lived at the time when the alphabet of the Phoenician traders was being adapted to the Greek language. He had the opportunity to do what none of his predecessors could do—put his poems down in writing. As the use of writing spread throughout Greece, so did the poems of Homer. Any Greek child who learned to read, learned to read Homer. Greeks prided themselves on knowing by heart long passages from the *Iliad* and the *Odyssey*, and Greek authors quoted Homer whenever they could, much as present-day authors quote the Bible or Shakespeare. Of course there was no printing in those days, so that each copy of Homer had to be written separately by scribes. It was only natural that mistakes crept into these copies. And since papyrus, the material made from an Egyptian plant upon which all texts were written, decomposed after a short period of time in the damp Greek climate, copies of Homer containing many variations were circulated.

THE ALEXANDRIAN SCHOLARS. The situation would have become intolerable had it not been for the efforts of a group of scholars in Alexandria, the city in North Africa founded by Alexander the Great, in the third century B.C. There, under the rule of Ptolemy I, a library was established for the purpose of collecting as many texts as possible of all the Greek authors. When the copies of the *Iliad* and the *Odyssey* were examined, it was discovered that they disagreed in many places. Lines that were present in some manuscripts were lacking in others. In some manuscripts episodes were expanded. Three scholars associated with the Alexandrian Library, Zenodotus, Aristarchus, and Aristophanes (not to be confused with the famous fifth century B.C. Greek comic playwright), worked to produce a standard text of Homer. Aristarchus, in addition to his work on the text, produced a commentary on Homer which deals with a number of critical points. Many other commentaries were written, ranging from complete works, published separately, to idle jottings in the margin of the text.

When parchment was developed, Homer's works, along with those of many other Greek authors, were transferred to this more durable substance. He was copied and recopied throughout the Middle Ages. The first printed edition of Homer was produced in 1488 by Demetrius Damilas in Florence, Italy.

OTHER EPICS. The *Iliad* and the *Odyssey* are only two of the many epics that were recited before the introduction of writing into

Greece. Of the others, only two have come down to us complete. These are *The Works and Days* and *The Theogony*, both attributed to Hesiod. Unlike the heroic epics of Homer, *The Works and Days* is didactic. That is, it has something to teach. In this poem Hesiod (who, unlike Homer, speaks in his own person) lists the tasks that have to be performed on a farm and the best days in which to do these jobs (hence the title). In *The Theogony* Hesiod presented, probably for the first time, a genealogy of all the Greek gods starting with the first, Chaos, and ending with the many minor deities.

We also have 33 hymns, none longer than 600 lines, many shorter than 30 lines. These hymns, addressed to one or another of the gods, Apollo, Aphrodite, Athena or Ares, have all, at one time or another been attributed to Homer, although we now know that some of them were composed as late as the third century B.C. They are still conveniently referred to as the Homeric Hymns.

THE EPIC CYCLE. The *Iliad* and the *Odyssey* are only two stories that revolve about the Trojan War. We know of other epics, now lost, that fill out the story from the judgment of Paris to the tale of Telegonus, a sequel to the *Odyssey*. Our main source for these epics is Proclus, a grammarian of the second century A.D. who summarized their plots in his *Chrestomathy*. These stories form the Epic Cycle and are as follows:

1) *Cypria* (named after Cypris, another name for Aphrodite). This epic, written by either Stasinus or Hegesias, opens on Olympus where Zeus and Themis, the goddess of custom, are planning the forthcoming Trojan War. Hera, Athena, and Aphrodite dispute among themselves which of them is the most beautiful; they choose Alexander (Paris) to be the judge, but he chooses Aphrodite solely because she promises that he can marry Helen if he judges in her favor.

Aphrodite directs Alexander to build ships to take him and his comrades to Sparta, and orders her son Aeneas, a Trojan, to accompany him. After learning of the future from his brother Helenus, Alexander sails to Sparta, stopping first to visit with Helen's brothers, Castor and Polydeuces. Menelaus sails to Crete, foolishly leaving Helen behind with Paris. She and he waste no time in getting together, and they set sail for Troy after filling the boats with treasures from Menelaus' storeroom. They sail through a storm stirred up by Hera and reach Troy, where they are married.

When Menelaus learns what has occurred, he returns home and plans a punitive expedition against Troy with his brother, Agamemnon, and Nestor, the oldest reigning king in Greece. They travel through Greece gathering a fighting force. (Odysseus pretends to be insane, so that he may avoid leaving home, but he is found out by Palamedes, who has accompanied Menelaus.) When they are assembled in Aulis, the incident of the sparrows and the snake that is described in Book II of the *Iliad* takes place.

They start out for Troy, but a storm disperses the ships, and they are forced once more to gather in Aulis. (Achilles' ship is driven to Scyros, where he marries Deidameia; he then rejoins the fleet in Aulis.) Before their second departure, Agamemnon angers Artemis, the goddess of the hunt, with his boast of his hunting prowess. She keeps the fleet in Aulis by means of strong winds until Calchas, the prophet, suggests that Agamemnon appease her with the sacrifice of his daughter Iphigeneia.

The Greeks set sail again and this time reach their destination, although they lose some time when they decide to leave Philoctetes, who has been bitten by a snake and has developed a smelly, festering wound, on Lemnos. Some of the battle scenes are described in which Achilles plays the major role. Zeus plots to have Achilles withdraw from the fighting.

2) *Iliad* of Homer. The *Iliad* continues where the *Cypria* ends.

3) *Aethiopis* by Arctinus of Miletus. The action of the Trojan War is continued from the point where the *Iliad* ends. Achilles kills Thersites for having insulted him. Later, Achilles is killed by Paris with the aid of Apollo. Aias and Odysseus argue over which of them should have the armor of Achilles.

4) *Little Iliad* by Lesches of Mitylene. In this epic the arms of Achilles are awarded to Odysseus. Aias becomes mad and commits suicide. Diomedes brings Philoctetes to Troy; healed by Machaon, he goes into battle, where he slays Paris. Epeius builds the wooden horse. Odysseus then disguises himself as a beggar so that he may enter Troy undetected and plot with Helen the taking of Troy (this episode is narrated by Helen in Book IV of the *Odyssey*). This epic ends with the Trojans' taking the wooden horse into Troy.

5) *Sack of Troy* by Arctinus of Miletus. The trick of the wooden horse succeeds: Troy is taken and the long war is over. Priam is slain by Neoptolemus, Achilles' son.

6) *Returns* by Agias of Troezen. In this epic are related the home-

comings of all the major Greek generals except Odysseus, whose return is thoroughly detailed in the *Odyssey*. Nestor and Diomedes arrive home safely; Menelaus reaches Sparta only after losing five ships. Agamemnon arrives safely in his native land, but is slain by his wife and cousin.

7) *Odyssey* of Homer. After many travails and travels, Odysseus reaches Ithaca, where he must slay a pack of suitors who are wooing his wife.

8) *Telegony* by Eugammon of Cyrene. This is a haphazardly planned continuation of the *Odyssey* wherein Odysseus indulges in many adventures and even marries again, although his wife Penelope is still living. Telegonus, his son by Circe (see Book X of the *Odyssey*), comes to Ithaca to find Odysseus and unwittingly kills him.

THE BACKGROUND OF MYTH AND IDEA IN THE *ILIAD*

The *Iliad*, like every other Hellenic literary work, epic or tragedy or comedy, must be understood not only in relation to a specific historical period, but also against the intellectual, religious and philosophical assumptions inherent in that particular period. Thus, knowing the conventions and principles of the Homeric world helps in large measure to clarify the motivations and actions of major characters such as Achilles, Hector and Agamemnon. Of course, there is much in the attitudes and ideals of the world of Homer that has relevance for us today, indeed, for all time. That is why the *Iliad* is such a universal work. Plato called the *Iliad* "the Bible of all Hellas" and that was a good four centuries or more after the traditional date of Homer's lifetime (8th cent. B.C.).

Perhaps the modern reader will find it difficult to see at first glance what is so profound about the *Iliad* and how it can be called "a Bible." For many, the *Iliad* seems to be a bloodthirsty work reveling in death (note the particularly gory descriptions of death Homer gives) whose hero is a childish sulker who causes great distress among his comrades because a slave-girl is taken away from him. In no way does Achilles seem to be a character one might identify with or admire. On the surface, his story warns against the consequences of uncontrolled anger and stubborness, but that in itself does not appear to be especially profound or complex. Yet the *Iliad* is one of the profoundest and most complex works created by man.

MYTHICAL STRUCTURE. Let us now consider in more detail the mythical structure leading up to and controlling in many ways the plot of the *Iliad*. Most importantly, the student must bear constantly in mind that a myth is not simply a "fiction" or silly fairy tale. While the nature of myth is a knotty intellectual and psychological problem we can safely say at least this much: very often myths are ingeniously symbolic constructions that are etiological, i.e., they explain the origin and creation of people, places, and things, or are projections in poetic form of man's own inner, troubled psychological life or again, are constructions that dramatize man's predicament in his relationship to himself, other men and the Universe in general. As such, while myths are not "scientifically true" they reveal, nevertheless, a poetic or philosophical dimension of truth to us that may ultimately be more significant for man than "scientific" truth. Sometimes, indeed, myth may be viewed as a substitute for scientific truth. For example, just as to us, today, so, to Homer's age, the true origins of the Trojan War were shadowed in mystery. Yet, an origin for the war was constructed. The story of this origin was touched upon in the *Cypria*—the story of the Apple of Discord. This story not only provides a substitute for historical causation but projects a vision of life vital to the early Hellenic or Homeric way of life and the *Iliad*. In this myth, Hecabe, Queen of Troy, dreams that she will give birth to a "firebrand" that will one day destroy her city. Thus, like Oedipus, the child she bears is exposed on Mt. Ida to die but is saved by a shepherd. The shepherd calls him Paris. Ultimately, after distinguishing himself, he learns of his identity and rejoins Priam. (In the myth Paris is not the feckless creature of the *Iliad*.) We then learn that at the marriage of Peleus and Thetis, the parents-to-be of Achilles— all the Gods are invited except Eris, the goddess of Discord, or Strife (which is what *eris* means). For the Homeric Greeks and throughout much of Hellenic history, *eris* was a concept that defined the nature of the universe. Everything in the universe existed, as it were, in a condition of opposites or contraries: Good—Evil, Love—Hate, Chaos—Order, Hot—Cold, Dry—Wet, Black—White, *etc.*, *etc.* In the plays of Aeschylus, for example, there is a powerful theological attempt to reconcile opposites (as in the *Oresteia*) and to create a "good" *eris*, a balance or harmony between opposing elements that produce strife or discord or disharmony. The "bad" *eris*—very often the naturally violent or chaotic conditions of life itself—reigns unchecked or is uncheckable at times and therefore creates tragic circumstances which dominate men. In this particular myth, Peleus and Thetis ignore Discord and so are ultimately punished by it; men cannot, *should* not—avoid trying to come to terms with Discord. Quite innocently, then, Paris is drawn into the web of fate that forces him to choose the fairest among the goddesses Hera, Athena and Aphrodite. Hera offers Paris sovereignty over Asia, Athena fame in war—power and fame—the two tantalizing ideals of the *Iliad*. But Paris, as we have seen, like most men chooses an immediate good—love. Thus Aphrodite leads Paris to Menelaus at Sparta which leads to the abduction of Helen which, in an Age dominated by a code of Honor, leads to war. War, then, becomes the absolute social manifestation of *eris*, a discord which is at once inevitable because that is the very structure of the world, i.e., "war" or strife is considered inherent in reality. Note, too, that men are partially responsible for the consequences of *eris* either because they fail to deal adequately with it by Reason and Law or because they submit to the *eris* within themselves, creating even more *eris*, as Achilles does in Book I of the *Iliad*. The overall impression of the myth suggests clearly the helplessness of men in relation to the powers outside themselves, the inexorability of fate and strife and man's weaknesses which contribute to *eris*. Finally it reveals the ideals and values to which he aspires—often tragically. In short, a vision of life is presented that is dominated by inexorability, strife, and the ideals of power, fame and beauty or love. Here is the world of the *Iliad*, philosophically shaped by the myth. One thing should be clear by now. The mythical explanation for the original of the Trojan War, is, in one dimension of thought at least, as "true" as any economic or military accounting for the war. The myth goes beyond the transient and "local" reasons for war and constructs a permanent and universal framework for human events.

MOTIVATING IDEALS. We can now turn to a discussion of the motivating ideals of the men who lived in such a universe. How did they come to terms with it? How did they fashion their lives? We must have at least a general idea of how to answer these questions if the *Iliad* is to be more than a "war novel." For the aristocrats of the Homeric Age—the men who did the fighting, thinking, idealizing—there were certain values and qualities by which men might wrest from an uncompromising universe of *eris* some measure of meaning and pleasure. These values were embodied in an Honor Code that defined and gave form to the lives of the aristocrats of Mycenae and Troy. First of all, a man was nothing if he did not have *timé* (tee-may), i.e., the esteem of his fellow-aristocrats. Most action was directed either to achieving or maintaining this esteem or honor. One of the ways a man might attain or increase his *timé* was to obtain glory (*kudos*). Glory was itself largely obtained in war—though not always—there were the great councils where a man's eloquence might prevail, or he might be a great poet. Of course, war was a condition where a man might bring *all* his powers to bear so as to win glory (as well as wealth). For Homer's heroes a man's *areté* (ar-ee—tay) was the key to his achievement. *Areté* is loosely translated as *excellence*. The word is, in fact, the superlative of the word *aristos* meaning "best." But the word implies more than excellence. It implies a kind of *power* a man has which does the excelling. A man's *areté* is that power within him which enables him, as it were, to transcend himself in acts of great excellence whether it be in spear-throwing or debating. Each *aristo*crat, therefore, strove to develop his *areté*, to realize completely the potentialities of high achievement he was born with. The more completely a man could excel in human activities, the more *areté* he had to have. A man could achieve so much *areté* that, in a sense, he ceased to be human and became almost god-like. This certainly is what happens with Achilles, Diomedes, Hector, Aias and others at various times. In fact, when a hero gives a great display of his *areté* we have an *aristeia,* an exhibition of a hero's valor, strength and skill.

THE ILIAD

As a result, an individual book of the *Iliad* that centers on one particular hero's actions is called, for example, the *aristeia* of Diomedes, or Agamemnon.

OBSESSION WITH GLORY AND HONOR. At this point we may ask ourselves why the Homeric Greeks were so obsessed with achieving glory and honor through high, god-like excellence, and with a system of values that is the very essence of a Heroic Age. While the question admits of no definitely ascertainable answers, a tentative answer may be put forth, an answer that receives support from the text of the *Iliad* itself and that carries a certain logic with it. In the first place, the ultimate purpose of so much glory and *timé* was to achieve for the hero *immortality*. Homer's world was a world where death was the ultimate fact of man's reality. There was a conception of a shadowy Hades to which he might go after death but it was gloomy and meaningless. In the *Odyssey*, Achilles, in Hades, tells the visiting Odysseus that he would rather be a live servant than a dead master. This is an ironic reversal of his attitude in the *Iliad* in which he had chosen a short life with glory to a tame longevity. This choice which creates Achilles' destiny or *moira* is in some ways the key to the question of death and immortality. Achilles' choice reflects the "heroic" choice, the choice which affirms that life is nothing in itself without glory. Yet, glory functions to negate death because a *man is remembered*. Thus, a hero can achieve a kind of immortality through his deeds in war. Of course, the more *areté*, the more *kudos* and, therefore, the greater the chance of being remembered and obtaining immortality. Death had to be faced and along with it the loss of earthly pleasures. But if it had to be faced as the end in an absolute way, then at least a man could face it heroically and in his own limited way, gain his immortality. This, clearly, is Achilles' motive for making the choice that defines his life and, therefore, his presence in Agamemnon's army in a war about which he really cares little except as a means to achieve glory. And Achilles is the central figure and the archetypal hero of the *Iliad*.

Understanding this, Achilles' action in Book I and the actions of many of the heroes in the *Iliad*, the war itself perhaps is more profoundly motivated for a modern reader. There is not just a city and loot to be gained, but immortality itself. And if a man loses *timé*, if he loses his impulse to win glory, he loses his chance for immortality. Achilles does not sulk and cause the tragedy he does out of mere peevishness; for him, as for Agamemnon, there is something more at stake: eternal fame. Indeed, this was the one way man could approximate the gods, who, as Phoenix tells Achilles in Book IX, "have greater *areté* than men." Not only did the Homeric hero wage a war against other men for glory and immortality, but he waged it against the eternal powers, the gods themselves.

Keeping this complex philosophical and mythic framework in mind, will make the action and ultimately the meaning of the *Iliad* become not only clearer to the reader but also more vitally significant to him. One or two more final reflections should be considered before plunging into an analysis of the *Iliad*. It should be kept in mind that the world of the *Iliad* is a tragic world for the most part because of the terrible irony its characters are involved in. And that is, that in order to achieve their immortality the heroes had to place themselves in situations of the greatest danger and therefore frequently of death. Ironically, the very evil the Homeric hero sought to overcome (as men do in different ways in all ages) became a constant companion to him: death. For it was mainly in war that the hero sought fame and brought himself closer to his end. Apart from Odysseus, for whom notably there is no *aristeia*, as for Diomedes, let us say, most of the great Homeric heroes do not survive the war. Some die, as Agamemnon after the war, because of something they did to bring about the war. This tragic irony lies at the heart of the *Iliad* and the reader should follow its course from the beginning.

ROLE OF THE POET. Finally, the role of the poet in all this must not be forgotten. Homer is singing of the *klea andron*, the glorious deeds of men. The great detail Homer lavishes on his heroes and the world they live in—a fact that blazes throughout every page of the *Iliad*—is part of the equation that leads to immortality. Keep in mind constantly that it is the poet who ultimately confers immortality on the heroes. That, indeed, is one of the functions of this great epic. We remember Achilles today because Homer sang of his destiny, and such an end is precisely what the Homeric hero sought.

BOOK I

THE PLAGUE AND THE WRATH

COMMENT: The first word of the *Iliad* is *menis*: This is usually translated as "wrath" or "anger." This wrath is to play an important role in the *Iliad* and is thus put into a prominent position just as the *Odyssey*, which revolves about the adventures of Odysseus, starts with the word "man." Many centuries later, Virgil imitated this initial stress by starting his epic, the *Aeneid*, with the words *arma virumque*, "arms and the man."

The opening line is also similar to that of the *Odyssey* in that it contains an invocation to the muse of lyric poetry. While, in both epics, Homer asks the muse to relate the story, the invocation is really a prayer that his memory and ability to compose an epic will not fail him.

The story of the *Iliad* begins with Chryses, a priest of Apollo (the archer god) from the city of Chryse. He comes with many gifts with which he hopes to induce the Greeks to release his daughter, Chryseis. (Remember: Chryses, the priest; Chryseis, his daughter; Chryse, his city.) She had been seized when the Greeks raided Chryse and had been given to Agamemnon, the leader of the Greek forces, to be his mistress.

Chryses addresses all the Greeks but directs his plea most strongly to Agamemnon and Menelaus. Everyone but Agamemnon is in favor of releasing Chryseis and taking the generous ransom Chryses has offered. However, Agamemnon tells the priest rudely to return home without his daughter and not to come back. As Chryses returns home along the seashore, he prays to his god, Apollo. He calls him by the rarely used name of Smintheus and asks him to unleash his arrows upon the Greek forces.

COMMENT: It is believed that "Smintheus" is an ancient Cretan title meaning "the mouse god." The reason why Chryses should address Apollo with what seems to be a demeaning title becomes clear when we see the results of his prayers: the Greeks are felled by Apollo's arrows. This is the poetic way in which Homer represents the plague that overcomes the Greeks, plagues which were frequently carried by mice. Another, more important consideration relating to the plague is that its occurrence reveals the ultimate victimization of men by the gods. For the gods produce situations which are very often out of all proportion, in terms of death and destruction, to the infractions of men against them, such as forgetting a sacrifice or, as here in the case of the *Iliad*, insulting a priest. The whole question of divine justice, of the proper and just relationship between crime and punishment, is here dramatized. Throughout the *Iliad* we shall see that *dikê* or Justice generally operates in a savage, vendetta-like fashion, the "way of nature," so to speak. There may be a balancing out between extremes, as often does occur in nature, but more often innocent men find themselves baffled and destroyed by powers beyond their control. Many centuries later, Aeschylus, in his great work the *Oresteia*, dramatized the change from this primitive *dikê* to a more moral, modern sense of justice which involves the notion of righteousness as inherent in the law. But in the *Iliad*, *dikê* is still a kind of "natural law," primitive in most aspects. In this instance, the Greeks are horribly punished, as we shall see, for one man's abuse of a priest. Retaliation is swift. But it is not only swift: it is all-encompassing and creates conditions which bring men into personal crises, crises that set off, chain-like, one tragedy after another. The opening statement of the *Iliad* contains the phrase "the will of Zeus," and this reflects the Greek belief that man is in the grip of forces he cannot control. "The will of Zeus" is another way of saying that all things are fated and out of the hands of man. Similarly, the Greeks referred to the *moira* of a man, or his portion in life, and to *anangke*, or final destiny and fate inherent in the nature of things.

The problem, of course, is complicated at once by man's own nature. We have emphasized "wrath," the human characteristic or flaw which begins the *Iliad*. Now we see Agamemnon acting rashly and sacrilegiously to Chryses. And yet the anger with which both men act can be justified, to an extent, on the basis of their honor code. A situation is created which brings out the worst in a man, despite his rationalizations. And the constant rationalization of the Greeks in facing tragedy was that, no matter how much guilt a mortal may be responsible for, the gods, or "the will of Zeus," is ultimately responsible. Thus, the whole matter of the plague in relation to those affected by it is of the utmost concern in the *Iliad*. It is both symbol and instrument. It symbolizes the morally distorted and tragic relationship men have to the gods, and it is instrumental in shaping the conditions which *necessarily* set the Greeks to arguing, therefore creating the whole ensuing tragedy.

For nine days, the plague rages over the Achaean camp, killing men and animals. On the tenth day, Achilles calls the warriors to an assembly. He proposes that Calchas, the prophet, be called upon to tell why the plague has befallen them. Calchas, who knows the cause of the plague, asks that no harm come to him for what he is about to say, for, he explains, it will make a great king angry. Achilles promises him protection even if he blames Agamemnon for the plague.

> **COMMENT:** Achilles' personality becomes clear immediately. It is he, rather than any other Greek general, who calls the assembly. He is also ready to pit himself against Agamemnon, even though Calchas has not (as yet) named him.

Thus reassured, Calchas reveals that it is Agamemnon's refusal to Chryses to release his daughter that has brought this destruction to their camp. Agamemnon arises angrily and accuses Calchas of always being the bearer of evil. He does, however, agree to return Chryseis to her father although he now demands a new prize; his honor would suffer if he, alone of all the Greeks, was to have nothing to show for his plundering.

COMMENT:
1) It is thought that, when Agamemnon refers to Calchas's bearing of evil prophecy, he is referring to the incident (as told in the *Cypria*—see the general introduction) in which the Greek fleet was stranded on the way to Troy. At this time, Calchas prophesied that the success of the venture depended upon the sacrifice of Iphigeneia, daughter of Agamemnon. Homer, however, does not mention this episode anywhere. (It is told by Euripides, a later Greek playwright, in his *Iphigeneia in Aulis*.)
2) Note that Agamemnon refers to Chryseis merely as a "prize," classifying her together with weapons and cattle. These prizes were the booty taken from the towns nearest to Troy which the Greeks had sacked for supplies. Thucydides, a Greek of the fifth century B.C., thought that it was the constant need to search for supplies which, in causing part of the Greek fighting force to miss the battle, enabled the Trojans to hold out as long as they did.

Achilles once again takes it upon himself to speak for the Greek forces and reminds Agamemnon that all the prizes have already been distributed. He asks that Agamemnon be patient and wait for the next raiding expedition. Agamemnon threatens to take a girl from another Greek general, Achilles, Aias, or Odysseus. (This threat is, of course, aimed at Achilles more than the other two. They have, with the rest of the Greeks, been keeping prudent silence.) Achilles is now raging with anger; he accused Agamemnon of being the greediest of the Achaeans and of always grabbing the best prize for himself. He says that he will return home rather than stay as a dishonored man.

When he sees that Agamemnon is intent on taking his mistress, Briseis, away from him, Achilles almost draws his sword to slay him. Athena appears, however, (visible only to Achilles) and bids him to control his wrath. He refrains from drawing his weapon but continues with his insults. He throws down his speaker's sceptre and sits down.

COMMENT: This is one of the most famous scenes in the *Iliad,* and one of the most significant. It is a miniature allegory in which Reason (Athena) controls Wrath (Achilles). This basic struggle between Reason and Passion became a fundamental theme or question for Greek philosophers and playwrights, particularly Euripides (see his *Medea* or the *Bacchae*). Later, in Book IX, both Agamemnon and Achilles will ascribe their great quarrel to *Até,* a word which is often translated as Folly, a lamentable impulse, or Ruin. But, at this instant, both men are struggling to maintain their *timé* (see Introduction) before the others and so assume full responsibility; later they will say the gods sent *Até* down to befuddle and destroy them. Thus, there is an ever shifting movement from personal responsibility to divine responsibility and back again. Who or what was finally responsible for a man's destiny remained the most important and yet most tragically insoluble question for the Greeks. After Sparta's victory over Athens there was, as Gilbert Murray phrased it in his *Five Stages of Greek Religion,* a "failure of nerve." Instead of Reason being enthroned as the highest concept of Greek philosophy, *Tyche,* Chance or Accident, ruled. But we must not forget that the Greek passion for Reason, so magnificently represented by Socrates, received its first approving dramatization in this scene.

Yet the reader must also be aware of an irony in this scene. For, while Reason triumphs, it does so only to create another tragic situation. Achilles will now decide to withdraw from battle, alienating himself from his comrades and the honor code they mutually share. And this withdrawal will cause more suffering for both Trojan and Greek than if he had killed Agamemnon on the spot, an act which, while tragic for the two men, would probably have forced the Greeks to return from Troy and end the war. But Achilles' *moira* is something else; his destiny is glorious death in battle.

Now Nestor, the aged king of Pylos, arises to speak. He chides the two warriors for their conduct, remembering that when he was their age warriors conducted themselves with more decorum, that is, they listened to his advice. He advises Agamemnon not to take Briseis, Achilles not to stay angry. Agamemnon praises Nestor for his advice, but says that it will do no good, for Achilles will not listen. Achilles repeats his intention of withdrawing from the fighting and promises to put up no resistance to Agamemnon's taking of Briseis.

The assembly breaks up. Achilles returns to his hut with his friend Patroclus; Agamemnon sends Chryseis back to her father under the care of Odysseus, the crafty king of Ithaca. A sacrifice of bulls and goats is made to propitiate Apollo, after which Agamemnon carries out his threat to Achilles by sending two heralds to bring back Briseis.

The heralds, Talthybius and Eurybates, approach Achilles in fear. But Achilles allows them to escort Briseis, telling them that it is Agamemnon, not they, at whom he is angry. Now Achilles goes alone to the seashore where he cries, calling to his mother, Thetis, who is a sea nymph. He laments that Agamemnon has dishonored him.

> **COMMENT:** Achilles is still the warrior he always was, yet his honor can be taken away by such a minor matter. The Homeric hero's conception of honor was based on the opinion of the people around him, and not on his own opinion of himself. Even though Achilles knows that he is still the greatest of the Achaeans and that honor is due him, he remains withdrawn from the fighting lest he seem to accept and acknowledge the dishonor.

Thetis comes to him and asks him the cause of his grief. Achilles replies that she already knows (since she is a goddess), but proceeds nevertheless to tell her what grieves him. He asks her to seek aid for him from Zeus, the leader of the gods. He reminds her of her claim that Zeus is indebted to her for having helped him when the other gods planned to kill him. She had brought a beast with a hundred hands, Briareus, to stay by Zeus's side, thereby frightening off the revolt-minded gods. Achilles wants Zeus to aid the Trojans so that the Greeks, pushed back to the sea, will realize how much they need him. Thetis says that Zeus is at present among the Ethiopians (considered by the Greeks to be the most distant of peoples) but that when he returns, twelve days hence, she will supplicate him, asking that he do what Achilles desires.

COMMENT: Thetis has a most important speech here that we must examine. She says, bursting into tears, "Was it for this I nursed my ill-starred child? At least they might have left you carefree and at ease beside the ships, since Fate has given you so short a life, so little time. But it seems you are not only doomed to an early death but to a miserable life" (Rieu translation). Note that she says that Fate had given Achilles a short life. We are told later, however, that a short life with glory was Achilles' *choice*. What is being said, of course, is that one's choice becomes one's Fate; they become merged. But what Thetis sees and proclaims here is the essence of Achilles' personal tragedy. He has chosen an early death in battle for glory, the only reason why a man would choose death over life in his heroic context. But if the glory is shorn away, then the choice becomes absurd, a mockery. And this is what Agamemnon has done to Achilles. He has stripped him of his chance for glory by forcing him, through the dishonor of taking away the prize which is the symbol of his honor in battle, to withdraw. Achilles' anger has, of course, contributed to this bad situation. But the real tragedy is not Achilles' alone. Everyone is involved. One man's actions inevitably have terrible consequences on all of society. This is certainly the larger tragic issue in the *Iliad*, though Achilles himself looms ever larger as an archetypal figure who tragically acts out in his own life a course based upon the complexities and contradictions in the honor code of his entire society.

The scene shifts to Odysseus' ship, which has now reached Chryse. Odysseus hands Chryseis over to her father and asks that a sacrifice be performed. Chryses, overjoyed to have his daughter back once more, leads the sacrifice, praying to Apollo for an end to the plague. The sacrifice lasts until the night, causing Odysseus, who, like all Greeks, preferred to sail by day, to put off his departure to the morrow.

For the next twelve days, Achilles remains by his hut, not going into battle. Thetis now leaves her home in the sea to go to Mount Olympus, the home of the gods, to fulfill her promise to her son. She approaches Zeus in the traditional manner of the suppliant, clasping his knees with her left hand, touching his beard with her right hand. Zeus hesitates, but finally accedes to her request. After Thetis' departure, Hera, Zeus's wife, approaches him, asking what evil counsel he has been plotting. He refuses to tell her, but to no avail for she is able to guess what Thetis wanted of him. Zeus tells her to sit down and keep quiet unless she wants to be hurt.

Sadly, she sits with the other gods gathered on Olympus. Hephaestus, the god of craft, tries to comfort her. He reminds her of Zeus's anger and how Zeus, once when angry at him, had taken him by the foot and thrown him off Olympus. Hephaestus now pours nectar for the gods. His clumsy lameness makes the gods laugh, thereby relieving the tension, as they see him performing the task usually reserved for pretty young girls and boys. The book ends with the end of the day.

COMMENT: It is most important to notice the behavior of the gods here. We see them playing favorites with no sense at all of any of the moral or even strictly political issues involved in the war. Zeus, while he can and does assert himself, is often nagged by Hera, and the others often behave as dissolute, unfeeling members of a rich family who are "above it all" in more ways than one. They have no compassion for an affliction of even one of their own, which implicitly heightens our idea of what their concern for man must be. Their attitude, in general, is one of bemused indifference to mortal tragedy though, and this is the best man can receive, they do sometimes show an angry if passing concern for one of their favorites when he is having a bad time of it. Book I ends with the development of a situation which will cause tragedy to countless humans. This has been spurred and instigated largely by the gods' terrible vindictiveness against humanity, only partly by man's own tendency to irrational behavior or carelessness in worshipping the gods.

We have seen how Book I began with a plague and a quarrel and how it ends with the gods laughing the night away. One might say that it begins with a tragedy and ends with a comedy and, indeed, this dramatizes the overall situation: man, beset with his own problems, is further distressed by the lashings of a universe, and the powers within it, essentially hostile or indifferent to him. Book I also develops three main structural or plot lines which the reader should follow throughout the *Iliad*, plot lines that are interrelated thematically and make the *Iliad* a unified work of art. These are: 1) the personal tragedy of Achilles; 2) the war between the Greeks and the Trojans, a social tragedy; 3) the relationship between the gods and men, a cosmic or universal tragi-comedy.

BOOK II
THE DREAM.
THE CATALOGUE OF SHIPS

Zeus alone of the gods does not sleep, but plans how the Greeks may be defeated. He sends a dream to Agamemnon that promises victory over Troy if Agamemnon attacks with his men. Agamemnon, deceived by the dream, at dawn of the next day sends forth his heralds to summon the Achaean host to an assembly. But before all the men assemble, he discusses the matter with his generals. He tells them of his dream, but, he says, before he leads them in battle, he wants to test the soldiers' desire to fight: he will offer them the chance to flee Troy. He leads the generals to the assembly where the men have gathered.

COMMENT: Now follows the first simile of the *Iliad*. A simile is a comparison of the form "like...so...." Here the Achaean soldiers are compared to bees swarming and buzzing. Homer frequently makes use of similes to relieve the morbidity of the battle scenes. Thus there are four times as many similes in the *Iliad* as in the *Odyssey*, where there is a greater variety of action; in the *Iliad*, there are four times as many similes in battle scenes as in non-battle scenes. The subject matter of these similes usually represents the domestic life of Homer's time rather than of the time of the Trojan War. They frequently come at the start or close of an important episode. Although they "take us away from the action" of the *Iliad* in the sense that we leave the battle, they relate back to the action in a metaphorical sense, and should always be closely examined. By means of his similes Homer interweaves scenes of peace into the martial atmosphere of the poem, showing that thoughts of war must always involve thoughts of peace.

Agamemnon addresses the assembly holding his sceptre, which was made by Hephaestus. He reminds the Greeks that ten years of fighting have not brought them victory, even though they outnumbered the Trojans ten to one. He suggests that they leave Troy and return to their families in Greece. The men, not realizing that

Agamemnon has been deceiving them, break out in a run towards the ships.

Hera, who has been observing the assembly, does not want the Greeks to leave Troy. She sends Athena to hold them back. Instead of speaking to each of the Achaeans, as Hera had suggested, Athena speaks only to Odysseus, her favorite mortal. Odysseus, thus prompted, seizes Agamemnon's sceptre and, running through the crowds, persuades the leaders to return; the men of lower rank he beats into submission.

When the men are once more seated, one of them, Thersites, rises to speak. He is one of the few characters Homer describes in physical detail: he is extremely ugly, bow-legged, lame, stoop-shouldered and nearly bald—altogether a disagreeable-looking person. Yet he has something to say which sounds quite reasonable to us: speaking for the common soldier, not only of the Achaean camp in Troy but of all time, he complains that he is risking his life for Agamemnon, his leader, who gets the booty and the glory. He tries to encourage the men to do as Achilles plans to do—leave Troy to Agamemnon and anyone else who still thinks that the city can be taken. Hearing this traitorous speech, Odysseus immediately acts to forestall a second mass flight to the ships. He reproaches Thersites for insulting Agamemnon, who is a nobleman, whereas Thersites is but a common man. Odysseus threatens to whip him if he should ever again dare to speak against Agamemnon—and proceeds to whip him anyway with his sceptre, raising a welt on Thersites' back.

> **COMMENT:** Thersites, with his sensible analysis of the fighting and his reasonable suggestion, is out of place in a society where honor depends on the glory attained from fighting. The fact is accentuated by his great ugliness.

The Achaeans have no choice but to accede to Odysseus' wishes. Odysseus once more addresses the men. He reminds them of the prophesy that Calchas had made when they were on their way to Troy. A snake had appeared during a sacrifice and had consumed a sparrow with her eight children. Calchas interpreted this act as an indication that they would have to fight in Troy for nine years before they would attain victory. Now, Odysseus saays, in the tenth year the Achaeans are close to their goal; they should remain and fight.

Nestor relates another favorable omen from Zeus, and he too asks them to stay. Now that Agamemnon has tested the soldiers, he proceeds with the plan outlined in his dream—the preparation for an attack on Troy.

Agamemnon calls a council of his generals and prays to Zeus, who sent him a false dream. A sacrifice is performed and dinner eaten, after which Nestor suggests that the Achaean troops be marshalled. Agamemnon follows his advice and gives the order for the men to appear in battle array. They march to their positions, an impressive series of similes being used to describe them.

Homer once more invokes the power of the Muses, as he is about to list all of the Achaean leaders and the number of their ships.

> **COMMENT:** This is the famous Catalogue of Ships. It is of considerable value to archeologists trying to reconstruct the political geography of the time of the Trojan War. It is believed to have been composed in the late thirteenth century or early twelfth century B.C. and handed down in the epic tradition until Homer's time. Many of the cities listed were no longer known to the Greeks of the Classical Period. The catalogue, which lists the leading figures of the war and the number of ships they command, might seem out of place in a poem which begins in the ninth year of the war. Homer employs the catalogue as a device to introduce the chief warriors to us. By placing at the beginning of the *Iliad* the catalogue which properly should introduce the entire Trojan War, Homer extends the significance of the brief episode which he narrates.

The largest contingent of ships and men comes from Mycenae, the kingdom of Agamemnon and richest city in the Aegean area at that time. Agamemnon's contingent numbers one hundred ships; his men are the best and most numerous.

The Trojans, thanks to Iris, the messenger of the gods, learn of the Greeks' battle plans. They too marshal their troops and the troops of their allies.

BOOK III
OATHS. THE BATTLE OF ALEXANDER AND MENELAUS

The two opposing forces now move towards each other, the Trojans with shouting and a clanging of weapons, the Achaeans silently. A huge dust cloud is sent into the air from the feet of the moving men. Alexander—also called Paris—leaps in front of the Trojan ranks with a challenge to the Achaeans. This challenge is accepted by Menelaus, the husband of Helen, whom Alexander had taken from Menelaus' very house, thereby causing the Trojan War.

Alexander regrets his too hastily given challenge, and withdraws into the Trojan ranks. Hector, his brother and leader of the Trojan troops, reproaches him for his cowardly action. He accuses Paris of paying too much attention to lyre-playing and love-making. Paris accepts the reproaches against his willingness as a fighter, but defends his right to make love. He agrees to fight Menelaus and have the outcome of the war depend on the battle: whoever wins is to have Helen and the treasure that came with her from Sparta.

Hector communicates this plan to the Achaeans. Menelaus agrees and suggests that a black lamb and a white lamb be sacrificed to seal the truce between the Trojans and Achaeans. Both sides take off their armor as a show of good faith. Hector sends to Troy for Priam, his father. When Helen learns that Paris and Menelaus are about to fight over her, she leaves her chambers to go to the wall of Troy in order to observe the contest. There she meets Priam, who is sitting with seven of the Trojan elders. After nine years the sight of Helen still impresses them. They are *almost* willing to admit that the war was worth fighting over such a beautiful woman. But they would still send her away, if they could.

Priam invites her to sit with him and asks her to identify the Achaean heroes visible from the wall.

COMMENT: After nine years of fighting, Priam could be expected to know the Achaean leaders by sight. But this is a good place for Homer to introduce them to his audience. This episode is called the *Teichoskopia*, "The Watch from the Wall."

Helen identifies Agèmemnon, who is a head shorter than most of the others. Next she names Odysseus, who is a head shorter even than Agamemnon, though broader in the chest and shoulders. Odysseus, she says, is known for his cleverness. Antenor, one of the Trojans on the wall, once entertained Odysseus and Menelaus before the start of the war, and he testifies to Odysseus' skill as a speaker, although his appearance is not so imposing as Menelaus'.

She next points out Aias and Idomeneus, King of Crete. A herald now approaches Priam to tell him of the ensuing contest between Paris and Menelaus; he repeats Hector's request that Priam come to witness the pledging of the peace oaths. King Priam and Antenor leave immediately through the Scaean gates. The sacrifice of the lambs is performed while Agamemnon prays to Zeus, asking him to witness the oath: whoever is victor is to have Helen and all her possessions. Once the sacrifice is over, Priam leaves so that he may not have to witness the fight.

Hector and Odysseus mark off the area for the fight and pick lots from a helmet to determine who shall start. Paris and Menelaus carefully dress themselves with greaves (shin guards), corselets, helmets, and shields. Paris, who has won the lot, is the first to throw his spear, which is stopped by Menelaus' shield. Now Menelaus throws his spear with a force strong enough to pierce Paris' shield. It is stopped, however, by his body armor. Menelaus rushes in, brandishing his sword, which breaks on Paris' helmet; he starts to strangle Paris with Paris' own chin strap, but it breaks. Menelaus throws the helmet to the Achaeans but, when he turns towards Paris, he discovers that Paris has gone, having been taken away by Aphrodite, Paris' champion. Aphrodite transports Paris to his bedroom.

Aphrodite now fetches Helen to tend to Paris, though Helen at first hesitates. When she does go to his room, she reproaches him for his cowardly action reminding him of his boasts that he could defeat Menelaus in hand-to-hand combat. Paris weakly defends himself and asks that she go to bed with him, and she does.

COMMENT: This last scene with Paris, Helen and Aphrodite is a beautiful instance of Homer's ability to weave psychology into symbol and symbol into psychology. We can never know whether Homer was aware of all the implications of this scene, but the artistry is so consummate that meanings emerge from every line. First to be considered is the fact that we have all together the three characters who are responsible, at least as immediate causes (see the earlier discussion of *Eris*), for the terrible tragedy of war that the *Iliad* describes. What heightens the tragedy is this very, in some ways, comic scene. The irony involved results from the contrast between cause and effect. Paris is a pleasure-loving, "playboy" king or warrior, putting sexual appetite before the more "manly" heroics (to Paris, at least) of a Hector or Achilles. He fights Menelaus to be sure, but Aphrodite takes him out of danger by hiding him in a mist, a frequent device of the gods. The mist operates clearly as a symbol of deception and of the way the gods relate to men. Athena lures Hector to his doom by this same trick of the mist, as we shall see later.

But more important is the psychological relationship between Aphrodite and her two favorites. Aphrodite, sexual passion or desire apotheosized, is the controlling psychological factor of Paris' personality. His escape from Menelaus is as much the result of his physical need for Helen as anything else. One can theorize that for Paris, the war—and in this case his fight with his mistress' husband—stirs him erotically rather than martially. Thus the war leads him, as it does some men, more to the bedroom than to the front-lines of battle.

Having brought Paris to where he belongs, Homer shifts his attention to Aphrodite and Helen. But Helen, while properly awestruck by the goddess' beauty (another indication of the ultimate superiority of the immortals, for Helen herself is "incomparable"), turns on her divine patroness, for her admiration for Menelaus' truer manhood has been aroused. Psychologically speaking, Helen's wish to reject such patronage reflects a wish to repress her sexual instincts or, at least, to hold them in check. Realizing, however futilely, what tragedy and unhappiness erotic passion has caused, she sarcastically tells Aphrodite: "forget you are a goddess. Never set foot on Olympus again, but devote yourself to Paris." And again: "I refuse to go and share his bed again—I should never hear the end of it. There is not a woman in Troy who would not curse me if I did."

Helen, too, has her code of matronly virtue, betray it though she may. Here she makes an attempt to control her passions, something neither Achilles nor Agamemnon in a different context had succeeded in doing. One cannot stress too strongly how important a factor human passion is in this poem. The failure to control rationally human passions is shown to be at the heart of war, of personal tragedy, and of the divine vengeance resulting from man's arrogance before the gods. The tragedy is intensified because the gods—the personified powers in nature and man—aggravate or incite or create conditions that cause men to explode emotionally. In this scene, Helen makes a good effort to control herself, but Aphrodite does, in fact, cause an explosion. She turns on Helen "in fury" and threatens to desert her and hate her so that her end will be "miserable." The result of this, naturally, is that "Helen was cowed, child of Zeus though she was." The point here is that Helen, being Helen, cannot do otherwise than submit to what is, after all, her most intense emotional trait, the trait that defines her for all history. If Aphrodite is love deified, Helen is love incarnate. Indeed, if she had, hypothetically of course, gone against Aphrodite, she would not have been Helen, the archetype of female beauty and seductiveness.

Homer subtly has Helen continue to scold Paris and to praise Menelaus over him. But this only excites Paris the more: "never have I felt such sweet desire," he claims, as they go to bed. "Meanwhile," we are told, "Menelaus was prowling through the ranks like a wild beast..." The effect is tragicomic. The lovers are enjoying themselves, self-indulging in the one passion that has any meaning for them. Helen has tried to escape but could not. In their little room they make love "on a well-made wooden bed." In a moment they become impervious to what they have caused: men turned into wild beasts.

BOOK IV
THE BREAKING OF THE OATHS

Observing the battle are the gods on Olympus. Zeus tries to anger Hera: he tells her that although she and Athena are on the side of the Greeks, Aphrodite has won the day for the Trojans by saving Paris. He wonders whether the gods should strive to maintain the truce that exists between the Achaeans and Trojans or whether they should stir up more fighting. Athena and Hera both want the fighting to continue until Troy is destroyed. Athena, however, merely sulks while Hera is moved to words: how can Zeus consider having the Danaans leave before Priam and his children are brought to their death?

Zeus is grieved at the extent of Hera's hatred for the Trojan host. She would like, he tells her, to enter Troy and eat Priam and his children now. He gives in to her and agrees to let her have her way, even though Troy has always been a favorite city of his. Hera replies that if ever Zeus wants to sack her favorite cities—Argos, Sparta, and Mycenae—she will not interfere, if only he will allow her to destroy Troy. And anyway, she adds, she is his wife and sister and shouldn't have to ask his permission. She requests that he send Athena to start the Achaeans and Trojans fighting again, if possible making the Trojans appear as the first offenders. Zeus instructs Athena, as Hera requested. Athena obeys immediately, bounding down from Olympus in the form of a shooting star, which amazes the Achaean and Trojan troops. They interpret it variously as portending a resumption of fighting or divine confirmation of the peace.

> **COMMENT:** All unusual natural events were considered to be an omen from the gods. However, the omen's precise meaning was not always evident and, as in the present case, could be taken to mean two opposing things. (Another example of this view of nature is sneezes, which were regarded favorably by some and unfavorably by others.)

Athena, now in the likeness of Laodocus, the son of Antenor, approaches Pandarus, the leader of the Trojans from Zeleia (as indicated in the Catalogue of Ships in Book II). Athena convinces him that, if he were to shoot an arrow at Menelaus, he would win glory from the Trojans and gifts from Alexander. Pandarus falls victim to this folly and with great care lets fly an arrow at Menelaus.

> **COMMENT:** The importance of this act is indicated by the great detail with which Homer describes it. We learn the history of the bow, that Pandarus used a new arrow, that he hid behind other Trojans lest he be seen before the shot, that he prayed to Apollo, the god of archery. See the Critical Commentary for the significance of this and other such detailed digressions.

Athena, though she wants the Trojans to break the truce, does not want Menelaus to die. She sees to it that he is merely wounded. Agamemnon shivers at the sight of the blood staining his brother's thigh. He addresses him tenderly, blaming himself for having allowed the truce to be made, and promises that the Trojans will regret this act. Menelaus assures his brother that the wound is not serious. Agamemnon, still concerned, tells him to lie still until a physician can tend to the wound. He bids Talthybius, his herald, to summon Machaon, the camp physician. Talthybius hurriedly executes this order. Machaon carefully pulls out the arrow, sucks out some blood, and applies medications.

By now, both sides have rearmed themselves and are preparing for battle. Agamemnon rides in his chariot to the front line, where he spurs the Danaans on to battle. He has special words of encouragement for Idomenus, the King of Crete, who promises to fight hard. Next he comes to Aias, son of Telamon, and Aias, the son of Oileus (the two of them are known as the Aiantes; their Latin name is Ajax). After praising their leadership, he comes upon Nestor, who is marshalling his troops. Agamemnon tells him that he wishes Nestor's body had remained as spry as his spirit. He moves on to Menestheus, King of Athens, and Odysseus, who are holding back, waiting for other Achaeans to start the fighting. He reproaches them, angering Odysseus, who claims to be the foremost Achaean warrior. Agamemnon apologizes for his too hasty accusation.

Agamemnon next sees Diomedes and Sthenelus, who are also holding back from battle. Agamemnon reminds Diomedes of his father, Tydeus, who was renowned in his lifetime for his bravery. Diomedes, not having Odysseus' way with words, has no answer to give Agamemnon. Sthenelus, however, angrily defends himself and Diomedes, saying that they are better warriors than their fathers ever were. Diomedes chides his friend for talking back to their leader.

COMMENT: Here we see how Homer can characterize a person with very few words. From this brief episode Diomedes emerges as a modest warrior, respectful of his superiors. Odysseus, on the other hand, will always have a speech ready to defend his actions.

Once again the silent Danaans meet in battle the shouting Trojans, who are impelled by terror, fear, and hate. Antilochus, a son of Nestor, is the first to kill a Trojan, striking him in the head with his spear. Trojans and Achaeans rush in to fight over the fallen man's armor.

COMMENT: A slain warrior was always stripped of his armor. To the Greeks, it is a symbol of a hero's identity, and the stripping of armor from a body signifies complete victory.

Aias, son of Telamon, kills Simoeisius; Antiphus, son of Priam, casts his spear at Aias. The spear passes Aias by, striking Leucas, a friend of Odysseus. The slaying of his friend angers Odysseus, who rushes into the Trojan ranks, killing Democoon and driving back the Trojan forces. Apollo, a partisan of the Trojans, tries to stop their retreat, but without success. The Argives press on, killing any of the Trojans who fall behind.

BOOK V

THE ARISTEIA OF DIOMEDES*

* "Aristeia" is that inspired moment of valor that comes on occasion to several of the Achaean warriors.

Diomedes confronts Phegeus and Idaeus, sons of Dares, a Trojan priest of Hephaestus. Phegeus casts his spear, but misses, and is slain by Diomedes' spear. His brother escapes, as Diomedes takes Phegeus' horses and chariot. The Trojans are dismayed by his death. Athena warns Ares, the god of war, that they should leave the battlefield, lest Zeus become angry with them. But even without divine help, the Danaans press on.

Agamemnon kills Odius, chief of the Alizones. Idomeneus kills Phaestus of Tarne, whose corpse is stripped of armor. Menelaus slays Scamandrius, a famous hunter. Meriones, a nephew and companion of Idomeneus, spears Phereclus, the carpenter who had built the ships that took Paris to Menelaus' house. Meges kills Pedaeus, a bastard son of Antenor, catching him in the nape of the neck with his spear. Eurypylus cuts off Hypsenor's arm, and leaves him to die from loss of blood.

Diomedes is the hero of this battle as he cuts through the Trojan line of defense. Pandarus (who had first broken the truce by wounding Menelaus) tries to stop Diomedes, and succeeds in wounding him in the right shoulder with an arrow. He yells encouragingly to the Trojans. Diomedes, however, is not out of the battle yet: he has Sthenelus pull out the arrow, and he prays to Athena to give him strength. She returns to the battle to help him and to warn him not to shoot at any immortals but Aphrodite. Athena enables him to distinguish between men and gods. With his strength restored, Diomedes rushes at the Trojans like a wounded lion rushing at sheep. He slays Astynous, Hypeiron, Abas and Polyeidus, sons of Eurydamas, Xanthus and Thoon, sons of Phaenops (we learn that their cousins will inherit the estate that was meant for them), and Echemmon and Chromius, sons of Priam, who are riding together in one chariot.

THE ILIAD

Aeneas, a Trojan warrior, seeing the havoc Diomedes is causing, rushes to the side of Pandarus and asks him to try once more to slay him—although he says, "Be cautious, he may be a god in disguise."

COMMENT: Aeneas, the son of Anchises, a Trojan, and Aphrodite, is a minor character in the *Iliad*, but according to a Roman tradition, it was he who, after the destruction of Troy, led some survivors to Italy where his descendants founded the city of Rome. Aeneas' story is told in the *Aeneid* of Virgil, a Latin epic modelled on the *Odyssey* and the *Iliad*, written in the first century B.C.

Pandarus recognizes the Greek as Diomedes, but admits that the fighter might be a god in Diomedes' shape, since Pandarus thought that his arrow had killed the warrior. Pandarus regrets that he did not listen to his father's advice and take one of his many chariots into battle; instead, relying upon his bow, he has now merely wounded Diomedes, spurring him on to kill more Trojans.

Aeneas offers him his own chariot, which Pandarus accepts if Aeneas will serve as driver. Sthenelus sees them coming and urges Diomedes to escape from this formidable pair—which Diomedes declines to do. So confident is he of victory that he directs Sthenelus to seize Aeneas' horses after he has killed the two Trojans. Pandarus casts his spear, hitting Diomedes' shield. Now Diomedes hurls a spear which catches Pandarus full in the face, driving through his nose and coming out beneath his chin. Aeneas jumps from the chariot to prevent the stripping of the armor from Pandarus' corpse. Diomedes picks up a boulder (which, Homer tells us, could not be lifted by two men of his own day) and heaves it at Aeneas, breaking his hip bone. Diomedes throws a spear that would have killed Aeneas, had not Aphrodite, his mother, protected him with her robe.

Sthenelus, meanwhile, remembering Diomedes' instructions, has taken away Aeneas' horses and given them over to Deipylus. Sthenelus goes to rejoin Diomedes, who is in pursuit of the goddess Aphrodite. He lunges at her and manages to cut her in the hand with his spear. Ichor, which flows from the veins of the immortals, flows from her wound. With a scream she drops her son, who is caught by Apollo.

Iris escorts her away from the battlefield to Ares. Aphrodite asks for the loan of his chariot, so that she may hasten to Olympus, where she can ease her pain. Once there, she relates the story to her mother, Dione, of how she was wounded. Dione tries to comfort her by telling her of other immortals who have suffered at the hands of mortals: how Ares was kept prisoner for a year by Otus and Ephialtes (these two brash brothers also tried to reach the heavens by piling Mount Ossa on Olympus, and Mount Pellon on Ossa—for which attempt they were killed). And she speaks, too, of how Hera and Hades were wounded by Heracles, the son of Amphitryon. Dione heals her daughter with a touch of her hand.

Athena and Hera make believe they know nothing of how Aphrodite received her wound. They pretend that she was scratched by a woman's pin. Zeus tells Aphrodite that she is out of place in warfare and should leave it to Ares and Athena.

Back on earth, Diomedes, still furious, is trying to slay Aeneas, who is still under the protection of Apollo. Apollo creates a phantom in Aeneas' shape to divert the Argives. He then asks Ares to get Diomedes off the battlefield. Ares, in the shape of Acamas, a Thracian, exhorts the Trojans to rescue Aeneas. Sarpedon, a Lycian warrior on the Trojan side, reproaches Hector for not fighting as hard as he should and allowing the Trojans to be beaten back.

Hector reacts by urging his troops to turn and face the Achaeans. Ares, obeying Apollo's request, helps the Trojans. Aeneas, given strength by Apollo, rejoins the battle, gladdening the hearts of his comrades.

Two Danaans, Crethon and Orsilochus, are felled by Aeneas. Menelaus and Antilochus, a son of Nestor, rush to prevent Aeneas from stripping the corpses of their armor. After bringing the bodies back behind the Achaean lines, Menelaus returns and kills Pylaemenes, leader of the Paphlagonians. Antilochus slays Mydon.

Hector, backed by Ares and Enyo, the goddess of war, rushes up front. At the sight of Ares, Diomedes urges the Achaeans to retreat, keeping their face to the enemy. The Trojans are quick to press their advantage. Tlepolemus, an Achaean and son of Heracles (who was a son of Zeus), confronts Sarpedon, whose father was Zeus. The two, grandson and son of Zeus, cast aspersions and spears at each other. Sarpedon's spear kills its victim. Sarpedon, himself, is struck in the thigh.

Odysseus kills many men, but Sarpedon is taken to safety. Hector rushes on, slaying some Argives. Athena and Hera are displeased by the aid Ares is giving to the Trojans. They leave Olympus on a beautiful chariot of gold and silver and travel to Zeus, who is sitting off by himself on a mountain peak. They demand that he withdraw Ares from the battle. Zeus refuses to act himself but suggests that Athena deal with the war god. Athena and Hera, after leaving Zeus, arrive at the Trojan battlefield, where Hera, imitating the loud-voiced Stentor (the word "stentorian," "having a loud voice," comes from him), exhorts the Argives to stand fast.

Athena, meanwhile, has gone to the side of Diomedes, whom she encourages. The two of them climb into his chariot, Athena holding the reins, and ride toward Ares. Athena makes herself invisible, so that Ares sees only Diomedes approaching. The god of war thrusts at him, but misses. Diomedes' thrust is more accurate and he stabs him in the stomach. Ares lets out a scream that stuns all the men on the field, then flies rapidly to heaven, where he tells Zeus how he was wounded, blaming Athena for encouraging Diomedes.

Zeus shows him no sympathy, but rather accuses him of bringing this wound on himself for constantly indulging in warfare. Zeus does, however, bid Paeeon, the god of healing, to tend to the wound. While Paeeon is obeying Zeus' request, Hera and Athena return to Olympus in triumph.

BOOK VI

HECTOR AND ANDROMACHE

The battle rages on. Telemonian Aias slays Acamus (whom Aias impersonated in the preceding book—there is also a son of Antenor with the same name); Diomedes kills Axylus and his squire, Calesius. Euryalus, a chieftain from Argos, slays Dresus and Opheltius, and then slays the twin brothers Aesepus and Pedasus. Polypoetes slays Astyalus; Odysseus spears Pidytes, and Teucer, a half-brother of Telemonian Aias, slays Aretaon.

Meanwhile, Menelaus has captured a Trojan named Adrestus, whose chariot has broken down. He pleads with Menelaus to let him go, offering him a huge bribe. Menelaus, who is about to listen to his captive, is restrained from keeping Adrestus hostage by Agamemnon, who reminds him of how he was treated when Paris visited his house. Agamemnon wants every Trojan killed. Menelaus heeds his brother's advice and pushes Adrestus away from him so that Agamemnon can thrust his spear through his side.

Nestor calls to the Danaans to wait until the end of the battle before stripping the Trojan corpses of armor, thus enabling all the Achaeans to be fighting at the same time. The Trojans are hard-pressed now. Helenus, Hector's brother, approaches Hector and Aeneas and asks that they stop the Trojan retreat: they should circulate among the troops to raise their spirits. Afterwards, Hector should return to Troy to tell his mother, Hecabe, in the company of the other older women of Troy, to offer a finely woven robe to Athena. She should promise, also, to sacrifice twelve heifers a year to Athena, if only the goddess will keep Diomedes away from Ilium.

Hector quickly heeds his brother's advice: he marshals his men so that they turn and face the Achaeans; then he leaves the field of battle to go into the city.

While Hector is on his way to Troy, Diomedes confronts Glaucus, the son of Hippolochus. Before he casts his spear, Diomedes asks Glaucus who he is, for he has never seen him before, and he may

THE ILIAD 45

be a god. Diomedes has no desire to wound another immortal, for he remembers the story of Lycurgus, who had slain the nurses of the god Dionysus. Zeus struck Lycurgus blind for this rash act.

Glaucus replies that his lineage is of little matter: "The generation of men is like leaves; wind may sweep leaves to the ground, but others grow when spring comes. Thus it is with men." But he does agree to disclose his ancestry: Sisyphus begat Glaucus, Glaucus begat Bellerophon. Bellerophon had the misfortune to appeal to his queen, Anteia, who tried to seduce him. When Bellerophon refused, she went to her husband with the lie that Bellerophon had tried to force himself on her. The king, Proetus, dared not kill him—instead he gave him a folded tablet with secret marks that would cause his death when he handed the tablet to the Lycian king, as Proetus directed Bellerophon to do.

> **COMMENT:** This is one of the two passages in Homer's works that refers to writing. The description of the tablet agrees with actual tablets found in Knossos and Pylos which were written on in the Linear B alphabet (see Introduction).

When Bellerophon reached Lycia, he was entertained for ten days until he was asked to show the tablet to the Lycian king. When the king read the signs, he tried to send him to his death by ordering him to slay the Chimera, a monster with a snake's tail, a lion's head, and a goat's body. Bellerophon killed her, only to be given a second task: to fight the Solymi, a race of fierce warriors. Again, Bellerophon succeeded, and again was given another task: to fight the Amazons. The Lycian king set an ambush for him, in case he should return. He did return, and he slew the men waiting in ambush. The king now realized that Bellerophon was a mighty warrior, and he offered him his daughter's hand and half of his kingdom, both of which Bellerophon accepted.

Bellerophon begat Hippolochus; and Hippolochus begat Glaucus, and sent him to Troy. Diomedes casts his spear into the earth, refusing to fight with him, for Oeneus, Diomedes' grandfather, was once host to Bellerophon for three weeks, after which they had exchanged gifts of friendship—a friendship which extends to their grandchildren. Diomedes suggests that they not fight with one another, now or in the future, and that, to seal their friendship, they exchange armor.

> **COMMENT:** Diomedes makes the greatest act of faith in Glaucus that a Homeric hero can offer, for exchanging armor is equivalent to exchanging identities. Homer, however, cannot resist speaking in his own character by saying that Glaucus

was a fool to exchange his golden armor for Diomedes' bronze armor, a hundred oxen's worth for nine—a very commercial note.

Hector has now reached the Scaean gates of Ilium, where he is surrounded by the wives and daughters of the Trojan warriors. After leaving them, he meets his mother, Hecabe, who acts like any concerned mother: she tells him to rest while she brings him some wine. Hector, in turn, acts like a typical son in refusing to listen to her. Instead, he repeats Helenus' suggestion that she offer a robe to Athena with the promise of twelve heifers a year if the goddess will keep Diomedes away from Ilium. Hecabe does as her son asks, but gets an unfavorable response from Athena.

While the older women are praying, Hector visits Paris, who has not left his bedroom since Aphrodite put him there. He rebukes his brother for not fighting with the rest of the men. Alexander accepts the reproach and arms for battle. Helen blames herself for everything that has happened. She invites Hector to sit by her and rest. He declines, offering the exigencies of the time and occasion as an excuse.

He now goes to find his wife, Andromache, who, he discovers, is not at home. He learns from a maid that she has gone with their son to the city wall. There Hector finds her and his son Astyanax. (Hector had named him Scamandrus but everyone else called him "Astyanax," "lord of the city," in honor of his father.)

> **COMMENT:** Notice that, as Hector has gone through the city, the people he meets are progressively more closely related to him: first were the Trojan women, then his mother, then his brother, and now his wife and son. This ascendancy of relationships (which is repeated in Book IX) serves to intensify the emotional atmosphere.

Andromache pleads with her husband not to return to the war; she reminds him that it was Achilles (whom she does not realize has left the battle) who slew her father, mother, and brothers. Hector, she says, is now her father, mother and brother, as well as husband, and she doesn't want to lose him to Achilles.

Hector, of course, refuses to consider deserting his men. But, concerned as he is for the fate of his men, he cares even more for the fate of Andromache, should Troy fall, for she would be the servant of an Achaean in such an outcome. (Recall the fate of Briseis and Chryseis.) He reaches for his son, but Astyanax shrinks back in alarm at the sight of his father's shining helmet with its high horsehair plume. Hector and Andromache break into laughter. Hector removes his helmet and fondles his son.

COMMENT: This last scene is considered by many critics to be the most "human" and touching scene in the entire poem. There is, indeed, a fine and ironic contrast drawn between the two parents brooding over their destinies while their son reacts as any little child would. The artistic "rightness" lies in having the parents immediately forget their own woes and allow themselves to be diverted in so sentimental a way. The scene, of course, further draws the contrast between Hector and Achilles. Hector is a man who loves his child and wife and who can forget war when a little child cries. Andromache and Hector are instantly humanized in a way that no other character is in the *Iliad* save Achilles throughout and Priam at the very end. Hector is the family man, the defender of the city, hearth and home. Perhaps that is why he has always been a more sympathetic character than Achilles who, by contrast, is essentially a "loner," despite his close friendship with Patroclus. When he is hurt, he goes running to his mother. As for marriage, it has no weight in his consciousness. He seems more the estranged youth than the manly defender represented by Hector, but this, as we shall soon see, is a necessary part of his role as "questor," a searcher after truth.

Another thing to note is Hector's statement that "Deep in my heart I know the day is coming when holy Ilium will be destroyed . . ." We see here again the battle with irrevocable destiny that the individual has to fight—and lose. Hector *knows* Troy cannot win, but he must never *act* on that knowledge. And he does not. Caught in the turmoil of war, fooled by his temporary victories, he acts and later talks as if Troy will win. But in this instance, Homer lets us into his sub-conscious, so to speak. He knows the truth but his commitment to his social order and his sense of honor force him to fly in the face of it.

In this way, Homer creates a hero worthy and complex enough to be balanced against Achilles. The two heroes together represent two types of tragedy: Hector, the tragedy of a man who has all the good things in life but must lose them in the very act of defending them; and Achilles, the tragedy of the alienated hero, the man searching for everything, who, in finding it, as we shall later see, perceives that it was not worth the suffering.

BOOK VII

THE BATTLE BETWEEN HECTOR AND AIAS

The Trojans are pleased to see Hector and Paris enter the struggle once more. Paris kills Menesthius of Arne; Hector slays Eioneus; Glaucus, now wearing Diomedes' armor, spears Iphinous. Athena, witness to this Trojan advance, hastens from Olympus to help the Greeks, but is intercepted by Apollo. He suggests that they stop the fighting for this day. Athena says that that is what she had in mind, and asks him how he would accomplish the plan. Apollo suggests that Hector should challenge a Danaan to a fight, thereby allowing the Achaean and Trojan troops to enjoy a respite from battle.

Thus, Helenus, having learned of the god's plans through his ability as a seer, suggests to Hector that he challenge an Argive hero, while the opposing sides sit down. Hector is pleased at this plan. He steps between the two armies and signals to his men to sit down; Agamemnon follows suit. Hector stands between the armies and gives his proposal: he will fight any Achaean in mortal combat; only let it be agreed that, if he die, his body be returned to Ilium, after it has, of course, been stripped of its armor. In turn he will return the corpse of the Danaan if he should prove victorious.

There is no immediate reaction from the Achaeans: they have no objection to his proposal but nobody accepts the challenge. Finally, Menelaus volunteers although he knows that he is no match for the mighty Hector. Agamemnon stops him before he arms himself but he does not volunteer in his place. Old Nestor arises to try to shame one of the other Danaans into accepting. He reminds them of Peleus, the leader of the Myrmidons, who was very proud to be associated with the Argives. Once, when Peleus and Nestor were fighting together, Nestor accepted a challenge from Ereuthalion, chief warrior of the Arcasians. This was after all had refused the challenge. If he were young now, as he was then, he says, he would not hesitate to accept Hector's challenge.

COMMENT: By mentioning Peleus, Nestor reminds them of Peleus' son Achilles, who, if he were present, would not fear to stand up to Hector.

Nestor's rebuke has its desired effect. Nine Achaeans volunteer. Agamemnon, Diomedes, the two Aiantes, Idomeneus, his nephew Meriones, Eurypylus, Thoas, and, last of all, Odysseus. Nestor decrees that they should draw lots to determine who should fight Hector. Each man marks his own lot—this and the episode of Bellerophon (Book VI) contain the only Homeric references to writing—and puts it into a helmet. Nestor shakes the helmet until a lot flies out: it is Telamonian Aias'. He is excited at the prospect and tells his friends to pray to Zeus on his behalf in a way that the Trojans may not overhear. Then, he silently changes his mind abruptly: let them pray aloud.

They pray as he directs and Aias arms himself so that he presents an imposing picture when he goes forth. Even Hector quakes a little at the sight of him. When they are close to each other, Aias says that Hector will soon see what sort of warrior the Danaans can depend upon, even without Achilles, who is still not fighting. Hector replies that he is not so easily frightened. He casts the first spear, which can not pierce Aias' seven-layered ox-hide shield. Now, it is Aias's turn to hurl a spear; it misses Hector by very little. The fight continues with spears, rocks, and swords but the two are evenly matched. Finally, darkness ends the fight with neither the victor. Hector, suggesting an exchange of gifts, gives Aias his silver-studded sword and receives from him a finely-embroidered belt.

After dinner, Nestor proposes that the armies arrange for a truce on the morrow so that both sides may gather their dead for cremation and burial. In addition, Nestor says, the Achaeans should build a wall; thereby making sure that they will have a defense if the Trojans should ever push them back to their ships.

Meanwhile, back in Ilium, the Trojans are arguing over Helen; whether to give her back or not. Antenor is in favor of returning her to Menelaus. Paris protests that he will not give her up although he is willing to give back the possessions that he took with him from Sparta. He will even add to them from his own wealth but Helen must stay. Priam bids his herald, Idaeus, go the next day to Agamemnon to inform him of Alexander's offer and, Priam adds, let Idaeus ask Agamemnon if he is willing to declare a truce until the dead are cremated. (This is the very plan Nestor is at this same time proposing in the Achaean camp.)

When Idaeus presents the offer the next morning, there is a brief silence. Then, Diomedes recommends that the Danaans reject the offer of the goods since they will sack Troy soon and get them back anyway. The Achaeans agree with Diomedes and Agamemnon tells Idaeus to convey their rejection of the offer to Priam. They are, however, willing to accept Priam's offer of temporary truce.

> **COMMENT:** Agamemnon does not let it be known that he was about to propose the very same truce.

Idaeus reports back to Ilium. Both sides send forth men to sort and wash the corpses. By the next dawn, the bodies are ready for the funeral pyres. Over the Achaean pyre, the Greeks build the wall that Nestor suggested and, in front of it, they build a trench, lined with snakes.

Poseidon, who has been observing the construction of the wall, protests that its fame will overshadow that of the Trojan wall; he and Apollo had built this wall for Laomedon, Priam's father. Zeus assuages Poseidon's fears by telling him that, once the Argives leave, the sea-god can break the wall and cover it with dust.

While the gods have been talking, a shipment of wine has come for the Achaeans. They pay for their wine with bronze, iron and cattle. The books ends as all go to sleep.

BOOK VIII

THE SHORT BATTLE

COMMENT: Book VIII contains the second battle of the *Iliad*. The first spanned Books II through VII.

The book opens on Olympus where Zeus is addressing the assembled gods. He wants the gods to refrain from helping either side so that he can fulfill his promise to Thetis. He promises the greatest punishment—exile in Tartarus, the penal sector of the underworld—to any god who disobeys his order. He claims to have the power to beat all the other gods combined.

The gods have no wish to test his power. Athena acknowledges his command, although she regrets having to leave her favorites, the Danaans, to their fate. Zeus asks that she not be angry with him, then leaves Olympus in his flying chariot. He goes to Mount Ida, which overlooks Troy and the Achaean ships.

Now that the corpses have been cremated (and the Achaean wall built), the temporary truce is over. Both sides arm themselves and meet for battle. The fight goes on until noon without either side's gaining the advantage. But now Zeus holds up a balance, placing the fate of the Trojans on one pan, the fate of the Achaeans on the other. The Achaean side plummets towards the earth, sending the Trojan side towards the heavens.

COMMENT: Zeus' scale portends victory for the Trojans, at least in this battle, if not in the war. Zeus makes use of his balance once again in Book XXII, when he weighs the fates of Hector and Achilles, who are engaged in combat.

Thunder flashes from heaven, sending fear into the hearts of the Achaeans. All turn to run, even Idomeneus, Agamemnon, and Aiantes. Nestor, however, cannot retreat, for Paris has speared one of his horses, which, in its death throes, has panicked the other horses drawing Nestor's chariot. Diomedes sees that Hector is drawing near to take his life. He calls to Odysseus, who is running back to the ships, to help him to save Nestor. But Odysseus evidently does not hear Diomedes' call. He keeps running. Diomedes hastens alone to Nestor's side and bids him enter his chariot.

Hector now has to face Diomedes and Nestor together. Diomedes' spear catches Hector's charioteer in the breast. Hector retreats. The Trojans turn to follow Hector, willing to give up the advantage they now have. But Zeus hurls a lightning bolt before Diomedes' chariot, frightening the horses and thus stopping the pursuit of Hector. Hector and his men turn once again to face the Achaeans. Victory seems theirs as Hector urges them to chase the Danaans past the walls and set fire to the ships. Confident of victory, he has words even for his four horses, asking them to help him get Nestor's shield and breastplate.

This confidence rankles Hera, who asks Poseidon to help her stop Zeus from driving out the Danaans. Poseidon hesitates to interfere with Zeus' plan. Meanwhile the Trojans have crossed the trench and are fighting before the wall. Agamemnon rallies the Achaeans just as the Trojans prepare to set the ships on fire. His exhortations, backed up by the sight of an eagle with a fawn in its talons that it drops before the Achaean altar to Zeus, cause the Argives to regain their spirits. They drive back the Trojans.

Diomedes is first, followed closely by Agamemnon and Menelaus, the two Aiantes, Idomeneus, Meriones, Eurypylus, and Teucer, who hides behind the shield of his brother, Telamonian Aias, whence he shoots his arrows.

COMMENT: Teucer's manner is an un-Homeric way to fight. Archery, in the *Iliad*, is usually practiced by the Lycians (Pandarus, their leader, wounded Menelaus and Diomedes with his arrows), the Carians, and the Paeonians, all of which nations are allies of Troy. The only two Achaean archers mentioned are Meriones and Teucer. (Odysseus in Book X uses a bow but he has borrowed it from Meriones. In the *Odyssey*, of course, he shows that he has great skill with the bow and arrow.) Archeological evidence of Mycenean times (see Introduction) confirms Homer's accuracy in having the Achaeans making small use of the bow.

Teucer quickly fells eight Trojans, earning congratulations from Agamemnon, who promises him rich prizes when the Danaans sack Troy. Teucer replies that he needs no such inducement to fight better since he is trying his best; he can't, however, hit Hector. As he shoots at him, he does manage to hit companions of Hector.

THE ILIAD

including Gargythion, a son of Priam, and Archeptolemus, Hector's charioteer. Hector manages to stop Teucer by heaving a rock that catches him in the shoulder. Aias runs to protect his brother.

The Trojans push the Achaeans back to their ships. Hera, who has failed to persuade Poseidon to disobey Zeus' order to stay out of the fighting, now turns to Athena. Athena, recalling some of the many favors she has performed for Zeus, agrees to stand by Hera in helping the Danaans. The two goddesses leave heaven in their chariot through the gates attended by the Hours.

Their machinations have not escaped the notice of Zeus. He sends Iris to them with a warning that, unless they desist from their mission, he will throw them out of the chariot, giving them wounds that will take more than ten years to heal. Swift Iris catches them at the gates of heaven and gives them Zeus' message. Hera has no wish to test Zeus' sincerity. She turns the chariot around and re-enters heaven.

Zeus leaves his vantage point on Mount Ida and returns to Olympus. Athena and Hera offer him no greetings as he sits on his throne, but he knows what they are thinking. He gloatingly tells them that they did the right thing in turning back. Hera replies that they will obey him. Still gloating, Zeus tells her that the Trojans will advance even farther on the next day.

Back on the battlefield, the sun has just set, ending the hostilities for the day. Hector addresses his assembled men, telling them to keep fires burning throughout the night so that the Achaeans may not escape in their ships. Now that the Trojans command an area outside the town walls where they can spend the night, they let the old men of Ilium keep guard, thereby preventing a surprise attack on Troy in their absence. At dawn they will attack and, Hector says confidently, destroy the Achaeans. The Trojans stay up during the night tending the fires and thinking of victory.

COMMENT: Book VIII ends with one of Homer's greatest similes. In this simile, the Trojan campfires are compared to the myriad stars in the heavens which can be seen on such a rare, clear night when it appears as if "the infinite depths of the sky are torn open . . ." The sense of wonder at the infinite expressed in this simile reflects a more profound religious sense than that met in the sometimes comic handling of the gods, as at the end of Book I. But again, as so often in Homer, there is also irony. For, while the Trojans are now seemingly at the height of their power and success, it is, in fact, the beginning of the end. Hector's apparently justifiable optimism is balanced by the Greeks' despair. The Greeks will now be forced to go to Achilles and urge him back into the war, the subject of Book IX. Little by little the wheels turn that will, indeed, bring Achilles back again with a vengeance that utterly dooms the Trojans. At this moment, however, they seem to have repelled Destiny and Hector makes a poignant boast, not aware, at least consciously, of what he had said to Andromache in Book VI about the ultimate defeat of Troy. He says to his troops: "I wish I were as sure of immortality and ageless youth and glory like Athena's or Apollo's, as I am that this day will prove disastrous to the Argives." Immortality, ageless youth and glory—here, complete, was the yearning of the Homeric hero and, implicitly, his despair. For only the gods could have those three together. Man, of course, could have the third—glory, but his search for it led him, ironically, through war to death.

BOOK IX

THE EMBASSY TO ACHILLES

While the Trojans sit confidently around their fires, the Achaeans are taken by fear. Agamemnon has the men come silently to an assembly so that the Trojans will remain unaware of his plan. In a speech that is but a shortened version of the one he gave in Book II, he again suggests that the Danaans leave Troy. Instead of the noisy flight that followed his first speech, the men now sit in silence, not knowing whether or not he is testing them again. The first to speak is Diomedes, who denounces Agamemnon for suggesting flight. He accuses his chief of lacking courage, inviting Agamemnon to leave if he so desires, but affirming that Diomedes and Sthenelus will stay, even if they are the only two. Nestor and the rest of the Achaeans endorse Diomedes' speech. Nestor also suggests that sentries be placed along the wall, while Agamemnon asks the Achaean elders for advice.

Nestor's advice is followed, and soon he, in his customary long-winded manner, is addressing Agamemnon and the other elders. He suggests that gifts and an apology be offered to Achilles, so that he will forget his anger and rejoin the fighting. Agamemnon admits to being in error. He offers Achilles tripods, gold, copper cauldrons, race-horses, and seven captive women, including Briseis. Agamemnon adds that when the Greeks sack Troy, Achilles can take as much as he wants from the city. In addition, Achilles can choose one of Agamemnon's daughters to be his wife, and her dowry will be seven cities for him to rule over.

> **COMMENT:** The usual practice in Greece was for the husband to give gifts to his new father-in-law, although there are other examples to the contrary in both the *Iliad* and the *Odyssey*.

After listing the gifts, Agamemnon says, "Let him yield to me who am so much more kingly." Nestor applauds Agamemnon's generous offer. He suggests that Phoenix—Achilles' teacher—Telamonian

Aias, and Odysseus be sent to Achilles to plead with him to fight again. The Achaeans are pleased with Nestor's plan. After a libation, the three envoys set out for Achilles' hut. They find him singing and playing the lyre. With him is his friend Patroclus. Achilles greets them and bids Patroclus serve them wine.

It is not until they have dined that the purpose of their mission is mentioned. Aias nods to Phoenix, as if to signal him to speak—but it is Odysseus who, noticing the signal, speaks first. After he has praised Achilles' food, he outlines the Acheans' current predicament and asks Achilles to help them. Odysseus reminds Achilles of Peleus' warning when his son was about to go to Troy: Achilles, he had said, should hold his anger in check. Odysseus now repeats Agamemnon's offer, using the very same words. Then Odysseus asks Achilles to pity his fellow Achaeans, who would honor him greatly if he returned to do battle.

> **COMMENT:** Odysseus repeats Agamemnon's exact words up until the point where Agamemnon demanded that Achilles accept the offer; instead of this harsh demand, Odysseus prudently substitutes a plea for Achilles to take pity on his comrades.

Achilles' reply is long and angry. His first point is that there is no reason for him to fight, since a coward has as much honor as he. He lists all the towns he had captured from which he received a smaller share of the loot than Agamemnon. He asserts that he will refuse to let Agamemnon heap dishonor on him another time.

He recalls how, when he was fighting, Hector dared not venture beyond the Trojan gates. Now Hector is threatening their very ships with fire. Tomorrow, Achilles tells them, he will set sail for Phthia, his home, leaving the Achaeans to their fate. He rejects all of Agamemnon's gifts. The offer he rejects most vehemently is that of his daughter's hand in marriage. "Let him choose another Achaean (for his son-in-law), one more kingly than myself."

He reveals a prophecy given to him by his mother: if he stays in Troy, he will not live to return home, though his fame will be great. If he returns home, he will live long, but without the great honor he would have had. He now recommends that they all consider leaving, particularly Phoenix.

> **COMMENT:** Achilles has replied, not only to Agamemnon's offer as stated by Odysseus, but also to what Odysseus left unstated—that Agamemnon still is haughty and unwilling to recognize Achilles' honor. When Achilles says "Let him choose

someone more kingly than I," he is sarcastically stating what he thinks is Agamemnon's view of him. How accurate he is can be determined by the fact that he unconsciously used the same uncommon word that Agamemnon used in addressing the Achaeans: "kinglier."

Achilles, like the other Achaeans, believes in a sense of honor that is external. That is, it depends on what other people think of you, and not on any self-evaluation. When Agamemnon took Briseis away from him, Achilles remained the same person he always was, yet in the eyes of his comrades and in his own eyes his stature had been diminished.

While Achilles' sense of honor remains inflexible, his overall vision of life does not. His speech reveals a very definite and significant change of attitude concerning life in general and his own destiny in particular. For he comes to the conclusion that death—that fact which is inescapable—levels brave men and cowards alike: "death comes alike to one who has done nothing and one who has toiled hard." His position is much like that of Ecclesiastes in the Bible; "Vanity of vanity, all is vanity" ("vanity" meaning futility or meaningless). Achilles sees that his ideal of striving for glory may, perhaps, be futile because in death all men become nothing and there is no special destiny for the hero. Even if the hero does achieve immortality in the memory of man, he cannot enjoy it. For, after all, life is better than anything else in existence. He says: "For life, as I see it, is not to be set off, either against the fabled wealth of Ilium ... or against all the treasure that is piled up in Rocky Pytho ... cattle and sturdy sheep can be had for the taking; and tripods and ... horses can be bought. But you cannot steal or buy back a man's life, when once the breath has left his lips." Then Achilles tells of his great earlier decision to choose an early death with undying fame over a long, uneventful life. Clearly, for the first time in Achilles' mind, a "homecoming" and long life seem at least as good and (by implication in this context) much more desirable than "undying fame." Achilles is no longer sure, and we with him, that his original decision was ultimately the wisest.

With such an attitude, of course, what Agamemnon has to offer Achilles becomes absurd. Against the fact of death, what can tripods or women or even fame mean? Thus, the Greeks' most powerful and persuasive weapon fails. In a sense, reason fails. The embassy now has two "cards" left to play. Phoenix represents wise old age and nostalgic friendship, another powerful weapon with which to persuade, while Aias represents a long-time, much respected comrade-at-arms, a relationship that carries with it its own elements of obligation and influence. One theme, however, that all three stress is Achilles' pride. But the student should observe the different ways in which each member of the embassy presents his case. The entire scene becomes a very subtle and fascinating debate as Achilles, with profound clarity and sadness, fends off one speaker after another.

Phoenix says that if Achilles leaves, he too will go since Peleus had asked him to take care of Achilles at Troy. Peleus had befriended Phoenix after he was exiled from his native land for having slept with his father's mistress at his mother's request. Phoenix recalls how he used to cut Achilles' meat and hold his wine cup when the boy was too young to do it himself. He felt, he says, that Achilles was the son he could never have, for his own father had placed a curse on Phoenix that kept him childless. He asks Achilles to overcome his feelings of pride and anger, recalling a story of pride that is similar to Achilles'. At a time when the Curetes were besieging the city of the Aetolians, the king's son, Meleager, refused to take part in the battle because his mother had prayed for his death for having slain her brother. When the Curetes were close to breaking down the gates, the Aetolian elders tried without success to get him to return to the fighting. Then his father, Oeneus, tried, followed by his mother and sisters. Finally his wife, Cleopatra, in tears, pleaded with him to save the city. It was Cleopatra's prayer that moved him to drive back the Curetes, although he had waited so long that the Aetolians gave him no gifts and did not honor him fully.

COMMENT: Observe that, as in Book VI, when Hector goes back to Troy, there is an intensification of relationship: first the elders, then Meleager's father, his mother, his sisters, and finally his wife plead with Meleager. Note also that it is Cleopatra who effects Meleager's return to battle; and that it is Patroclus who, with his death, brings about Achilles' return to battle.

Observe, also, that just before telling his tale, Phoenix inserts a brief theological sermon. Even the gods, he says, allow themselves to be swayed if a miscreant sacrifices and prays to them. Prayers are the daughters of Zeus and they oppose sin (Até). As Phoenix explains it, there is a battle between Sin and Prayer and, unless men use prayer and act in the spirit of prayer (contrition, reasonableness, piety, *etc.*), Sin will win and bring great misery upon man. Indeed, if a man rebuffs the Daughters of Prayer, they ask Zeus to allow Sin to overtake that man and punish him. Phoenix next tells Achilles: "You must give their due to the Daughters of Zeus by letting them placate you as they do all noble hearted men."

Phoenix thus presents in symbolic form a sermon against pride, inflexibility and, finally, irrationality or foolish passion in general. The ironic justice consists in the fact that if a man behaves irrationally, irrational things will happen to him. Nature or the gods join in, as it were, to enforce his irrationality, thus precipitating the inevitable tragedy to follow. There is, on the other hand, the way of prayer, reason, balance, acceptance of forces greater than oneself, the knowledge of which gives a man pause before he acts and, most importantly, enables him to change his actions instead of clinging compulsively to one fixed way. We see Achilles again, then, as the central figure in the basic tension and conflict between Reason and Passion which was first developed in Book I.

Achilles' reply is most significant: "I have no use for the Achaeans' good opinions. I am content with the approbation of Zeus..." This means that Achilles is now rejecting an external sense of honor for an internal one. His thoughts on this matter have changed just as his whole vision of life has changed. Indeed, these great changes in Achilles, we may surmise, are the result of his forced withdrawal. He has been off-stage, to be sure, but forces are at work in him which will contribute more to the meaning of the *Iliad* than if he had been physically present at the front lines.

There is, however, a question as to whether his new concept of intrinsic honor is really an advance or, rather, a retrogression as far as his understanding and character are concerned. If we see it as an advance, we may liken Achilles to Socrates, who many centuries later refused to do anything merely to satisfy other people and who recognized only his own conscience as a guide to action. Thus we may say that it is not now the fact that the Achaeans did not honor him which is causing him to refrain from battle but that, for the first time, he realizes that he does not need their approval, that he maintains his true honor whether they know and signify it or not. On the other hand, by referring ultimately to Zeus for his justification, Achilles further widens the breech between himself and his comrades, creating a more profound alienation than had existed before. In another sense, then, Achilles may be adding to his "sins" or errors of spiritual insight by the very way in which his present level of insight causes him to divorce himself from his community and his obligation to it.

After Achilles has put down Phoenix, only Aias remains, and he turns upon Achilles in great anger: "I cannot help reflecting on the combination of rancour and arrogance that Achilles has displayed. Ruthlessness too. Not a thought for the affection of his comrades . . . The inhumanity of it!" Aias has not actually said anything substantially different from the others. It is only his language and tone which have been fiercer and even contemptuous. And it is this that touches Achilles and forces a slight concession from him: "I have a notion that, however furious his attack may be, Hector will be brought up short, here by my own hut and my own black ship."

Achilles can ward off any intellectual argument thrown at him, but emotional contempt from a man he admires breaks him down. This is one of Homer's most penetrating insights into human psychology. But again there is great irony attending this situation. Achilles will wait until the last moment to re-enter the war and no sooner. But his slight shift from his completely inflexible earlier position will cost him dearly. For, in the process of waiting until defeat for the Greeks seems inevitable he will send his dearest friend Patroclus to fight in his place. Patroclus will be killed and the war prolonged more days with more deaths just so that the point, both physically and emotionally, can be reached which will bring Achilles into the fight again. But when he does rejoin the fight, as we shall see, it is with the guilt of indirectly causing his best friend's death. In addition, when he does go back into the battle, this guilt will make Achilles behave like a monster. Thus his wrath and his inability to give in *completely*, as a rational man would do, project dire consequences for the future. The line of causation from book to book is drawn with clarity and insight. The "will of Zeus" is working.

Odysseus and Aias return to the camp where they tell of Achilles' refusal to fight. Diomedes is now sorry that they ever went to him, for now Achilles will be prouder than ever before. He suggests that they get some sleep in preparation for the battle to come—a suggestion that is quickly followed.

BOOK X

THE DOLONEIA

Agamemnon and Menelaus, unable to sleep, leave their huts and meet by the Argive ships, where Menelaus asks if Agamemnon plans to send a scout to spy on the Trojans. His brother tells him to summon Aias and Idomeneus while he calls Nestor. Agamemnon finds Nestor asleep in his hut. After Agamemnon awakes Nestor and asks his company on an inspection of the sentries, Nestor suggests that they also wake Odysseus, the Aiantes, Meges, and Idomeneus. "What about Menelaus?" he asks. "He shouldn't be sleeping at a time like this."

Agamemnon tells him that tonight Menelaus is not shirking his duty. The two of them now go to arouse Odysseus, who asks them why they are wandering about through the night. When he learns of their plan, he agrees to go with them. The next hut they visit is Diomedes', whom Nestor wakes up by kicking him with his foot. Nestor bids him summon Aias and Meges, the chief of Dulichium.

When the men are assembled, they make their rounds of the sentries, encouraging them to maintain their watch. They then discuss the situation. After an exchange of ideas, Nestor suggests that one of them spy on the Trojans and perhaps learn their plans. The stalwart Diomedes offers himself to be the scout, but asks that another go with him. The Aiantes, Meriones, Nestor's son, Menelaus, and Odysseus volunteer.

> **COMMENT:** Once again Odysseus is the last to volunteer, as he was when Hector challenged an Achaean (Book VII). It is by such means that Homer characterizes his minor characters.

Agamemnon leaves the choice of a companion to Diomedes, who chooses Odysseus, the wiliest and most adventurous of the Achaeans, as Diomedes goes on to say. Odysseus, who probably didn't want to go, cuts short Diomedes' praise, and the two set off to accomplish as much as possible before daybreak.

As they set out, Odysseus takes a heron's squawk to be a favorable sign from Athena. Odysseus prays to her to watch over them. Diomedes promises that if she helps them as she once helped Tydeus, his father, he will sacrifice a heifer to her.

Meanwhile, in the Trojan camp, Hector is addressing the leader of his army: he asks for a volunteer to scout the Achaean ships to determine whether or not they are planning to leave. The only person to volunteer is Dolon, not a handsome man, but swift-footed. He will do it, he says, if Hector promises him Achilles' horses and chariot when the Argives are conquered. After Hector promises him what he asks, Dolon sets off, wearing a wolf-skin over his shoulders and a weasel-skin hat.

Odysseus and Diomedes see Dolon coming towards the ships and realize his purpose; they allow him to pass them in the darkness and then give chase. Thinking that they are Trojans that have further instructions to impart to him, Dolon stops when he hears their footsteps. But he soon realizes who they are and starts running. For a time he eludes them, but is finally caught by Diomedes. Fearing for his life, Dolon pleads with them to take him alive and ransom him to his wealthy father.

Odysseus tells him not to let the thought of death disturb him (implying that they are not going to kill him) and asks him his purpose in spying on the Achaeans. Dolon tells Odysseus that Hector has promised him Achilles' chariot for information about the Achaean plans. Odysseus now asks Dolon for the layout of the Trojan camp; where Hector is, where the weapons are kept, how many sentries there are, etc. Dolon tells everything, including the fact that the allies of the Trojans are also present. Odysseus demands to know about them, too, and once more Dolon reveals what he knows, thinking that his life will therefore be spared. However, now that they have learned what they wanted to know, Diomedes strikes him in the neck with his sword.

Odysseus and Diomedes continue on their way to the Trojan camp with the knowledge of the deployment of the troops. There they find the white horses of Rhesus, king of the Thracians, about whom Dolon had told them. While Diomedes kills thirteen of the Thracians, including Rhesus, Odysseus unties the horses. The two of them now ride swiftly back to the spot where they had killed Dolon; they take his weapons and return to the camp.

Nestor is the first to notice their arrival and asks them how they obtained the horses. Odysseus relates the story of the slaying of Rhesus; then he and Diomedes wash themselves and eat.

BOOK XI

THE ARISTEIA OF AGAMEMNON

It is now dawn, and the third battle of the *Iliad* is about to begin (it will last through Book XVIII). The Spirit of Strife spurs the Achaeans to fight. Agamemnon carefully arms himself as the chariot-drivers prepare the chariots for battle.

On the other side of the battle line, the Trojans under Hector are also readying themselves for battle. Polydamas, Aeneas, and three sons of Antenor—Polybus, Agenor, and Acamas—are ready to serve as Hector's generals. As the two sides meet for combat, Eris, the goddess of strife, is the only immortal present, since the others are away in obedience to Zeus' orders. Even Zeus is merely an onlooker.

The battle rages through the morning with no advance made by either side. A break in the Trojan line is finally made when Agamemnon slays Bienor and his driver. Agamemnon now rushes after and kills Isus and Antiphus, two sons of Priam. The Trojans turn to run, as Agamemnon captures Peisander and Hippolochus, sons of Antimachus, who plead for their lives. But Agamemnon knows that their father had once proposed, when Menelaus and Odysseus entered Ilium on an embassy, that Menelaus be killed on the spot. Agamemnon kills them, then turns his attention to where the fighting is thickest.

It is not long before the Trojans are driven back to the gates of their city. Zeus decides to intervene: he sends Iris to warn Hector to yield to Agamemnon until Agamemnon is hit with a spear or arrow. Iris delivers the message to Hector, who orders his men to turn and face the Achaeans. But Agamemnon continues his slaughter, killing Iphidamas, a son of Antenor. Coön, his brother, tries to spear Agamemnon as he bends over Iphidamas' body to remove the armor. He succeeds in piercing Agamemnon's arm and proceeds to drag away his brother's body, but Agamemnon kills him with his spear.

Agamemnon continues to fight until the pain in his arm forces him to withdraw. Hector uses Agamemnon's retreat to spur on his men. Hector himself kills Asaeus, Autonous, Opites, Dolops, Opheltius, Agelaus, Aesymnus, Orus, and Hipponous. The battle is now in the Trojans' favor, until Odysseus and Diomedes take a stand and stop their advance when the battle is once more evenly fought.

Hector now directs his chariot towards Odysseus and Diomedes. The latter strikes Hector's helmet with a blow of his spear heavy enough to make Hector fall to his knees. Hector does, however, manage to climb into his chariot before Diomedes can recover his spear. Diomedes, who is stripping the armor from a body, does not notice that Paris is advancing towards him until Paris shoots an arrow through his foot.

Paris leaps from his hiding-place, gloating over the flesh wound he has inflicted. Not at all afraid, Diomedes threats Paris with contempt, abusing him for his curly hair and his lecherous manners. "When *I* shoot an arrow," Diomedes says, "it finds its mark." Under the protection of Odysseus, Diomedes pulls the arrow from his foot and rides back to the ships.

Odysseus, after some soul-searching, holds his ground, but is quickly surrounded by Trojans, like hunters carefully surrounding a wild boar that they dare not approach too closely. Odysseus keeps them at bay, killing any who come too close, although one of them, Socus, manages to wound him, at the cost of his own life. Menelaus and Aias, responding to his cries for help, rescue Odysseus from the Trojans.

At another place on the battlefield, Paris has just wounded Machaon, the physician to the Achaeans, whom Nestor takes away from the fighting. On the advice of his chariot-driver, Cebriones, Hector goes to the place where Aias is fighting, although he does not directly confront him. Seeing the forces arrayed against him, Aias slowly retreats, keeping his eye on the Trojan spearmen.

Eurypylus comes to aid Aias, but is almost immediately hit in the thigh by a spear of Paris. He makes his way back to the Danaans, ordering them to help Aias.

At this point Achilles looks towards the battlefield and sees Nestor driving the wounded Machaon to the ships. Since from such a distance he is not sure that it is Machaon, he sends his friend Patroclus to find out. When Patroclus reaches Nestor's hut, he finds him tending Machaon. Before he can leave, Nestor asks him why Achilles is so interested in but one wounded man, when so many

Achaeans lie wounded, including Diomedes, Odysseus, Agamemnon, and Eurypylus. In his usual, long-winded manner Nestor says that he has not the strength; otherwise the Achaeans would not need Achilles. He recalls an incident from his youth that won great praise from his father, Neleus, king of Pylos.

Nestor had fought the Eleans over some cattle and won a victory. Three days afterwards, when the spoils had been divided among the Pylians, the Eleans attacked in full force. Nestor was the hero of the ensuing battle. Thus Nestor puts himself forward as an example for Achilles.

He reminds Patroclus of what his father Menoetius had told him when he and Achilles set out for Troy. Peleus, Achilles' father, had just told his son always to be first in battle. Then Menoetius told Patroclus to be a good example for Achilles and to give him sound advice. Nestor asks Patroclus to act on his father's advice and advise Achilles to return to battle. If Achilles will not do so, let him at least allow Patroclus to fight, for, being rested, he may be able to drive back the Trojans.

Patroclus hastens to carry out Nestor's bidding, but is detained when he sees Eurypylus who has limped away from the battle with an arrow still stuck in his thigh. He asks Patroclus to tend to his wound. Patroclus agrees and asks him how Hector can be stopped. Eurypylus, however, can see only destruction for the Achaeans. Patroclus helps him to his hut and, taking the arrow from his thigh, washes the wound.

BOOK XII

THE BATTLE BY THE WALL

While Patroclus tends Eurpylus, the Trojans once more gain the advantage in the fighting, threatening the Achaean wall. Homer tells us that the wall will be destroyed by Poseidon and Apollo after the Argives leave Troy; the gods will direct the force of all the neighboring rivers toward the wall, while Zeus helps with rain from above, until the wall is reduced to the level of the ground.

But this is in the future. The wall still stands. Hector himself is described as being "like a tower," as he incites his men to leap the trench. To do so, they must dismount from their chariots and cross on foot. They cross the trench divided into five companies; Hector and Polydamus lead the largest contingent, with Cebriones as third in command. Paris, Alcathous, and Agenor lead the second company. The third is led by Helenus and Deiphobus, both sons of Priam. Aeneas and two sons of Antenor, Archelochus and Acamas, are in command of the fourth company. The fifth contingent, consisting of allies of Troy, is led by Sarpedon, Glaucus and Asteropaeus.

One ally, however, Asius, refuses to humble himself by fighting on the ground: he manages to get across with his chariot but, Homer reveals, he is doomed to die by Idomeneus' spear. He and his followers make their way towards the ships, but are stopped by Polypoetes and Leonteus, two Lapiths, who defend the ships with spears and stones. The Trojans, too, throw stones, but to no avail. Suddenly, an eagle appears, holding a crimson-colored snake in his talons, which turns and bites the eagle in the breast, causing the bird to drop the snake in the midst of the soldiers.

Polydamus tells Hector that Zeus has sent this omen to portend that, just as the snake fought as long as he was alive, so will the Achaeans fight, killing many Trojans. Hector rejects this interpretation of the omen, remembering Zeus' promise of a Trojan victory. He tells Polydamus not to tell anybody else of his interpretation.

Hector leads his troops in an attempt to break through the Achaean wall, but his troops are repulsed at every turn. The two Aiantes exhort the Danaans to fight their hardest while the Trojan stones keep falling on the wall.

Sarpedon advances on the Wall with his shield and two spears. He urges Glaucus to come with him and so win everlasting glory. The two go forward, with their Lycians following, towards the section of the wall guarded by Menestheus. When he sees them approaching, Menestheus calls to the two Aiantes, but the clatter of shields and spears drowns out his call for help. He sends his herald, Thoötes, to summon Telamonian Aias.

When Telamonian Aias hears Thoötes' message, he orders Aias, the son of Oileus, to remain with Lycomedes while he and his brother Teucer go to aid Menestheus. The Lycians have already arrived and are storming the wall when Aias and Teucer arrive. Aias kills Epicles with a rock, and Teucer shoots an arrow through Glaucus' arm.

Sarpedon grieves that Glaucus has to withdraw, but he continues his advance and is able to break off a section of the wall. Aias and Teucer direct all of their spears and arrows at him without scoring a blow. For a time the Argives manage to keep the Trojans from entering the breach in the wall.

Hector urges his men to press forward. He lifts a huge bolder and tosses it against a gate, breaking it. The first to rush through, Hector, then calls to his men to follow. They climb over the wall and run in through the gate. The Danaans flee to their ships.

BOOK XIII

THE BATTLE BY THE SHIPS

Having inspired Hector to break through the Achaean wall, Zeus turns away from the battle-scene and gazes upon distant peoples—Thracians, Mysians, Hippemolgoi, and Abioi.

> **COMMENT:** Homer interrupts the tense action with an abrupt contrast, evoking strange images: note that Hippemolgoi means "milkers of horses," and the Abioi are described as "most righteous of men." As the god turns to this unreal spectacle, there is stressed most poignantly the difference between the gods who cannot die and the suffering mortals who must.

Poseidon, however, contrary to Zeus' exception, does not wish to stop aiding the struggle of the Achaeans, and he strides from his perch on high Samothrace to his golden palace at Aegae, where he harnesses his team to his chariot. His horses have bronze hoofs and manes of gold. Attired in gold, Poseidon drives out over the waves, and the beasts of the sea rejoice in their master. Unyoking his chariot between the nearby islands of Tenedos and Imbros, he enters the Achaean camp, assuming the form of the prophet, Calchas. He exhorts the two Aiantes to resist Hector, and, touching them with his staff, he fills them with courage. As Poseidon disappears, Aias, the son of Oileus, recognizes him as a god by the back of his divine legs and by the regenerated spirit in his own breast.

Meanwhile Poseidon stalks among the ranks of the Achaeans, rousing their spirits as they stand terrified at the numerous Trojans who stream through the breach in the wall. "Shame!" he cries "that the best of the Argives should abandon the fight, when formerly the Trojans did not dare to stand up against the Achaeans." Poseidon blames the incompetence of Agamemnon, who has insulted their best warrior, Achilles, but appeals to the profound sense of honor and pride of the rest of the Danaans.

THE ILIAD

COMMENT: The hortatory, or encouraging, war speech, delivered by a general before battle, was a standard part of ancient warfare and served as the subject for brief lyric poems by poets such as Tyrtaeus, a Spartan poet of the seventh century B.C. Homer incorporates various examples in his poem.

The Argives, eager for the encounter, close ranks behind the two Aiantes and await the Trojans.

Hector comes on like a boulder hurtling down a rocky slope, but stops before the Achaeans like the stone when it reaches the level plain. His brother Deiphobus stands forth with him. Teucer opens the fierce battle by slaying Imbrius, the husband of an illegitimate daughter of Priam, but Hector prevents for the moment the stripping of his armor, killing the Argive Amphimachus. The Achaeans retrieve the body of their warrior, while the Aiantes bravely carry off Imbrius. Aias, son of Oïleus, in his fury severs the head of Imbrius and hurls it like a ball to the feet of Hector.

COMMENT: It must be noted that throughout this book the fight assumes a barbaric and bloodthirsty character which is not found in earlier battles. In the life and death encounter by the ships, it is blind force and primitive energy which prevail.

Poseidon, in grief at the death of his grandson Amphimachus, in the likeness of Thoas, accosts Idomeneus, ruler of the Cretans, who is tending a wounded companion. Idomeneus, inspired, dons his armor. He encounters his squire, Meriones, who is returning to replace a spear he has lost. They exchange statements on their own courage, each boasting of the Trojan spears he has retrieved in close combat. Idomeneus lauds the bold warrior, who never trembles or grows pale, and who, if he falls, is wounded in the chest, not in the back as he flees. He offers a spear to Meriones, and they head for the left wing of battle where the fighting is fiercest and where there is opportunity for glory. There the Trojans and the Argives clash in close formation.

As in a desperate tug-of-war, Zeus and Poseidon keep the battle moving to and fro: Zeus inspires Hector and the Trojans, and his brother Poseidon fights among the Danaans.

The old indomitable Idomeneus slays Othryoneus, who fought for the hand of Cassandra, the loveliest daughter of Priam, and taunts his body bitterly. He kills Asius, and then Alcathous, husband of Hippodameia, finest lady of Troy. Idomeneus then challenges Deiphobus, announcing his descent from Zeus through Minos, the famous king of Crete. Deiphobus appeals to Aeneas for aid, who supported by the noble Trojans, makes for Idomeneus, around whom gather Argive lords. Menelaus joins the fray and slays Peisander. Menelaus accuses the Trojans of breaking Zeus' laws of hospitality when they stole his wife and denounces their insatiable appetite for war. The battle on the left wing continues like an unquenchable fire.

> **COMMENT:** Idomeneus is the appropriate hero for this bloody fight. He is an old man representing an ancient kingdom, and his code demands a primitive fierceness where virtue lies in fearlessly meeting one's fate. Idomeneus does not seek to stand out before the ranks for personal glory, but fights grimly among his men. Note the harsh taunts.

At the center, the two Aiantes resist Hector's onslaught, with the son of Telamon standing at the head of his men; but the Locrians, the tribe following Oileus' son, stand behind, for they fight with the bow and sling.

On the advice of Polydamas, Hector seeks out the Trojan leaders for consultation. He learns of the rout on the left wing, blaming Paris in his anger. Paris and Hector together lead their ranks against the Argives. Hector and Aias exchange insults, and the book ends with the din of clashing armies.

BOOK XIV

THE DECEIVING OF ZEUS

Nestor, tending the wounded physician Machaon in his hut, is roused by the clamor and seeks to find out what is happening. He picks up the shield of his son, Thrasymedes, who had taken his father's shield, and steps outside to discover the broken wall and the rout of the Achaeans. He decides to seek Agamemnon, the commander-in-chief.

The wounded lords, Diomedes, Odysseus, and Agamemnon, meet Nestor as they come from the ships drawn up on the beach, in order to survey the battle. They use their spears as canes to lean upon. Agamemnon inquires why Nestor is leaving the fight, fearful lest Nestor should burn the ships as he had promised. Nestor reports the destruction of the wall and the invasion of the Trojans, suggesting that the kings take counsel, since wounded men cannot fight.

Agamemnon is typically despondent in bad fortune. He concludes that Zeus has granted Hector victory and urges that the Argives draw their ships into the sea and depart by night. It is better to run and remain alive, he offers, than to die when the gods are adverse. (Compare this speech with Idomeneus' attitude.)

The shrewd Odysseus reprimands Agamemnon's cowardice, urging that they fight to the death. Moreover, he is careful to note, Agamemnon's plan is a most stupid tactic, for the army will never stand steady against the enemy while the ships are being dragged into the sea: rather they will look behind them, and lose their spirit for the struggle. Agamemnon yields to Odysseus' superior reasoning, and requests an alternative plan.

Diomedes, the youngest hero of the *Iliad*, makes bold to offer a plan, accepting Agamemnon's invitation for advice. He modestly begs that they heed him despite his youth, and relates his proud lineage to demonstrate his worth, ending with dutiful praise of his father, Tydeus. He urges that, wounded as they are, the three should return to the battlefield, keeping clear of the turmoil so as not to receive a second wound. In this way they can encourage those who might be slack in the fighting.

The kings accept Diomedes' suggestion. Poseidon, in the guise of an old man, approaches Agamemnon, and, berating Achilles for staying out of the war, assures the chieftains of eventual victory. The god then speeds across the plain with the cry of nine or ten thousand warriors, rousing the spirit for battle in the ranks of the Achaeans.

Hera, wife of Zeus, who is happy about Poseidon's work among the Argives, spies Zeus who is sitting on the highest peak of Mount Ida, surveying the battle, and she devises a plan to divert his attention from the Trojan plain so that the Danaans may gain the upper hand with the assistance of the gods. Deciding to seduce her husband, she bathes in ambrosia and divine olive oil to increase her beauty. She dons a lovely robe which Athena had woven for her and puts on other trimmings which a lady wears, including earrings. Hera then begs Aphrodite to perform a favor for her despite the fact that their sympathies in the war are on opposite sides. Aphrodite agrees, and Hera invents a lie to deceive the love-goddess as to her purpose. She pretends that she will visit Ocean, the river that encircles the earth and the grandparent of the gods, and his wife Tethys, who have quarreled; she will reunite them with Aphrodite's power of love.

Hera travels from Olympus beyond the mountains of the Thracians to Lemnos, where she encounters Sleep, the brother of Death. She promises him a golden throne if he will put Zeus to sleep. Sleep replies that he is fearful of deceiving Zeus, the greatest of the immortals, recalling the time he cast slumber upon the god's eyes so that Hera could raise a storm against Heracles. Zeus raged bitterly and cast cold terror into Sleep, whom he would have brought to harm had not the god taken refuge with Night, whom Zeus was unwilling to offend. Hera finally induces Sleep to do her bidding with the offer of one of the younger Graces for him to marry. From Lemnos they pass to Gargarus, highest peak of Mount Ida, where Zeus in the form of a songbird sits amid the branches.

Zeus is filled with desire when he sees Hera and asks why she comes. She repeats the tale she had invented. Zeus, overwhelmed by her beauty, suggests that she postpone her task to another time, and he tactlessly compares her to all the women he has known in love. Hera, he concludes, is the loveliest. Hera's modesty compels Zeus to cast a thick mist around them, and flowers grow and lift them from the ground.

COMMENT: Note the harmony of the deities with the

forces of nature: when the gods engage in the act of procreation, the mountain blooms under a thick moist haze.

Sleep meantime delivers the news of the seduction of Zeus to Poseidon. The god leaps to the fore, exhorting the nobles and the ranks, advising that they pool their armor so that the best fighters may have the better weapons.

COMMENT: This unusual scene of a transfer of armor in the thick of battle is suggestive of a pooling of identities. At the moment of crises, individuals melt into the common entity of the tribe. If we fail to see the symbolism, we miss the poetry, and, like the great but literal-minded Homeric scholar, Walter Leaf, find only absurdity. He writes, "the suggestion of a change of armor in the hottest of the fight can hardly come from a poet familiar with real war ... The whole passage ... is a very poor addition."

Hector and Poseidon lead the opposing armies against each other.

COMMENT: Poseidon clearly represents the elemental force of battle, with perhaps a suggestion that it is the sea at the backs of the Argives which drives them forward. We are not to understand that Hector is so powerful or so irreverent as to give battle to a god, nor would Homer permit such an irrational encounter. The symbolic role of the deity is made sufficiently clear by the fact that he disappears entirely when the fighting begins, replaced by the Danaans for whom he stands.

The encounter of Hector and Poseidon raises a din louder than the waves on a beach, the crack of a forest fire, or the howl of a gale-wind.

COMMENT: Again the power of war is compared to elemental forces: the brilliant scholar and critic, Simone Weil, writes in her pamphlet, *The Iliad or the Poem of Force* (see bibliography):

"It is not the planning man, the man of strategy, the man acting on the resolution taken, who wins or loses a battle, battles are fought and decided by men deprived of these faculties, men who have undergone a transformation, who have dropped either to the level of inert matter, which is pure passivity, or to the level of blind force, which is pure momentum. Herein lies the last secret of war, a secret revealed by the *Iliad* in its similes, which liken warriors either to fire, flood, wind, wild beasts, or God knows what blind cause of disaster, or else to frightened animals, trees, water, sand, to anything in nature that is set into motion by the violence of external forces."

Hector makes a vain spear-cast at Aias, who flings in return a huge boulder at Hector which knocks him down. His men gather round him and bear him behind the lines to the river Xanthus where he painfully recovers and blacks out again.

The fight is renewed with greater vigor and even more bitter taunts. King Peneleos slays Ilioneus, an only child, and raises his severed head upon his sword, bidding that the wife and parents of the boy lament.

Homer appeals to the Muses to enumerate the dead, and the book closes.

BOOK XV

THE RETREAT FROM THE SHIPS

As the Argives chase the Trojans back beyond the trench and wall, Zeus awakes to see Poseidon routing the Trojans and Hector lying half-conscious. In anger he turns threateningly on Hera, rebuking her for her treachery. He reminds her of the time she drove Heracles in a storm to the island of Cos (see Book XIV), when he strung her in the heavens with anvils bound to her legs, and no one could rescue her. In terror Hera swears it was not she who prompted Poseidon to fight on the side of the Achaeans. Mollified, Zeus orders Hera back to Olympus to send Iris and Apollo to his side. Iris, the messenger, is to recall Poseidon from the fracas, and Apollo will be sent to revive Hector. Zeus then predicts the course of the remainder of the war: with the aid of Phoebus Apollo, Hector will rout the Achaeans, driving them back to the ships. Achilles will dispatch his friend and squire, Patroclus, who will fight bravely and kill Sarpedon, son of Zeus, but Hector will destroy him. Achilles in his anger will slay Hector in return, and the Trojans will be driven back until, with the help of Athena, Troy will be taken. But in the meanwhile, he will give glory to the Trojans, in accordance with the promise he made to Thetis to honor Achilles.

Hera, in the instant that it takes for one to imagine it, speeds to Olympus. She accepts a chalice offered by Themis, the goddess of order and customs of mankind, and announces that Zeus has bitter plans for the gods and goddesses partial to the Danaans. She laments that Zeus' great strength prevents the other immortals from seeking satisfaction, while he sits apart serenely unperturbed. She also bitingly reports to Ares that Ascalaphus, his son, has been slain. In a rage Ares hastens to arm and orders his henchmen, Demos and Phobus ("Fear" and "Panic" or "Rout") to harness his chariot.

Athena, however, in terror for the Olympian host, lest everyone suffer the wrath of Zeus, dashes after Ares, tearing away his helmet, shield and spear, and vehemently orders him to abandon his mad intention. She leads him back into the hall, and Hera delivers her message to Iris and Apollo.

The two deities fly to Zeus on Mount Ida, where Iris is ordered to bid Poseidon retire from the battle, lest he be forced by Zeus, who is mightier and older than the sea-god.

Iris drops to the plain like hail and delivers her message to Poseidon. The Earth-shaker is infuriated; he points out that the sons of Cronus and Rhea were three: Zeus, Poseidon and Hades. They cast lots for the realms of the universe. Zeus received the heavens as his portion, Hades the underworld, and Poseidon the seas, while the earth was left common to all of them. Let not Zeus presume to give orders to his equals.

> **COMMENT:** The concept of seniority is an important theme in the *Iliad*. Recall that Agamemnon's stature is attributable to his greater age and authority, although Achilles is the more powerful. Achilles challenges Agamemnon for kingship. The gods, who are more tradition-minded, respect the authority of the eldest. Note that Zeus is called "the *father* of gods and men," never "the *king* of gods and men." Zeus is thus seen as the chieftain of a clan, whose rank is insured by his birthright.

Zeus next tells Apollo of Poseidon's retreat—it is better, he says, than for such gods to come to combat—and gives Apollo the aegis with which he is to terrify the leaders of the Achaeans. He must inspire Hector with such boldness that he will reach the ships of the Danaans. Apollo obeys and finds Hector regaining consciousness, for now Zeus has willed his recovery. Apollo inquires what has happened to Hector.

The hero recognizes that a diety is with him (who naturally knows all), but he explains that Aias felled him. Apollo breathes courage into Hector, who bounds like a stallion back to battle. The Danaans retreat in panic at the sight of him. But Thoas, king of the Aetolians, counsels that the multitude should return to the ships, while the most valiant warriors impede the charge of Hector. With Apollo in the lead, the Trojans advance. So long as Apollo holds steady the aegis, both sides hold fast their positions, but when the god brandishes the tassled aegis and emits a piercing cry, the Danaans flee in terror, and the Trojans pick them off as they run. Hector threatens to kill any man in his army who lags behind the pursuit in order to collect spoils.

Apollo kicks down the edges of the ditch, making a passageway over which the Trojans may cross. He smashes the wall on which the Achaeans had expended great labor like a child crushing sand castles.

> **COMMENT:** The transitory nature of man's works is most strikingly expressed in this simile. The destruction of the Achaean wall suggests the razing of the wall of Troy, which takes place after the poem's conclusion. One purpose of the *Iliad* is to show that man's importance lies not in the futile constructions of his hands, but in the process of struggle itself.

Nestor prays that Zeus may protect the Argives and is rewarded with the omen of a thunderclap, which inspires the Trojans to fight more fiercely, for they suppose the token is meant in their favor.

Patroclus, still tending Eurypylus, is roused by the cries of the fleeing Danaans, and decides to hasten to Achilles, that he may try to persuade him to intervene in behalf of his allies.

The combat rages at the ships, with Hector and the greater Aias in the thick of conflict. Hector kills Lycophron, and Aias calls the bowman Teucer to his assistance. Teucer hits Cleitus, and aims next at Hector, whom he would have killed, but Zeus causes his bowstring to snap, and the arrow wanders harmlessly. Aias and Teucer realize that the gods have deserted them, but resolve to fight staunchly with their spears.

Hector too perceives the will of Zeus, aware that the fates are on his side, and he urges all to attack. If any man should fall, he says, it is no dishonor to die for kin and country. Aias for his part delivers a hortatory speech to his men. After much slaughter, Hector urges Melanippus, a cousin of the slain Dolops, to protect Dolops' body with him. Menelaus sparks the courage of Antilochus, son of Nestor, to dart forth and bring down Melanippus. Antilochus retreats before the onslaught of Hector after killing his man.

Now Zeus spurs Hector on to set the ship ablaze, using the Trojans to honor the wrathful Achilles. Hector himself is the instrument of Zeus, who grants him glory, for he is soon to fall beneath the attack of Achilles. Like a flame or a tidal wave, Hector attacks and, killing only the valiant Periphetes, he turns the Danaans to rout. Nestor urges the Achaeans to remember their reputations and their families and to stand firm against the enemy.

Aias, with a long pole, protects the ship of Protesilaus, from which he fights, holding off the Trojans, who struggle mightily under the leadership of Hector. The Trojan prince at last grabs the prow and, holding fast, he calls for a torch to set fire to the vessel. Aias, weary and under continual attack, slowly backs off, slaying twelve men, and ever exhorting the Argives to fight bravely, for there is no ally behind them, no room to retreat, but the battle is for life or death for the Achaean host.

BOOK XVI

THE PATROCLEIA

Patroclus, weeping at the fate of his comrades, arrives at the tent of Achilles. Achilles inquires what the matter might be, that he cries like some little girl trailing behind her mother, begging to be picked up. He asks whether some bad news from home has reached Patroclus. Perhaps their fathers have experienced some evil—but of course Achilles knows that news from home is not the reason. And then he suggests that Patroclus may be grieving for the Achaeans, who are suffering what they deserve for permitting Achilles to be dishonored.

Patroclus reports the misery of the Argive army and the injuries which the great kings have sustained—Diomedes, Odysseus, Agamemnon and Eurypylus. He berates Achilles for his intractable vengefulness, thanking heaven that his own spirit is not so pitiless. Achilles, he cries, is not the son of Thetis and the noble Peleus: he is the child of the sea and hard crags.

> **COMMENT:** Patroclus' image contains a play on words. Thetis is a sea-nymph, while Peleus, the name of Achilles' father, resembles Pelion, the name of a famous mountain in Magnesia in ancient Greece. Punning of this sort was not considered trivial by the Greeks, but rather names were held to have intrinsic meaning for the people to whom they were attached. (Compare lines 1080-82 of the tragedy *Agamemnon* by the Greek playwright Aeschylus, where the name of Apollo, who plays a hostile role, is associated with the word *apollumi*, which in Greek means to "destroy.")

Patroclus asks whether some prophecy or sign keeps Achilles from the struggle. He then implores Achilles to let him lead the Myrmidons into battle. The sight of fresh forces might drive the Trojans back for a while and give the Achaeans a much-needed respite. He also begs that Achilles permit him to don his lord's armor so that the Trojans will take him for Achilles and will shrink back in confusion at the sight of the formidable hero.

Homer interrupts the narrative to predict the impending doom of Patroclus.

Deeply disturbed by Patroclus' plea, Achilles answers that he knows of no prophecies which hold him back. It is the cruel insult of Agamemnon who, by virtue of his greater authority, dishonored him by seizing the prize that Achilles had won and that was due him. Yet Achilles is willing to forget the past, he does not desire to maintain the feud, yet he has vowed not to re-enter battle until his own ships have been attacked. He bids Patroclus put on his famous armor and lead the Myrmidons against the pressing foe, for the ships must be protected. Yet, he warns, let not Patroclus presume to storm Ilium, but rather let him return to Achilles when he has driven back the Trojans. Let him not take the honor away from Achilles by gaining victory without him.

> **COMMENT:** This speech gives profound insight into Achilles' problem. He has long desired to return to the side of his comrades, to take his rightful place among the lords in the great struggle and terminate his self-imposed excommunication. Yet he is still unable to act as a member of society, the dynamic living force within him is yet in chains, his excuse is his vow; Achilles has not yet learned to renounce absolutes. One part of Achilles, however, does respond: his pity for the Achaeans, his kindness. These qualities in Achilles are represented by Patroclus, who is always gentle. Patroclus goes to war in Achilles' armor, and thus in Achilles' place. When Patroclus dies, all mercy will leave the heart of Achilles, who will emerge as pure violence and energy.

Aias, meanwhile, can no longer bear up under the furious attacks of Hector and the Trojans. Homer asks the Muses to tell how fire is first brought to the ships: Aias's pole is lopped off by Hector's sword, and, defenseless, he is forced to yield. The Trojans ignite the prow of the ship.

Achilles is roused to action. He assembles his men. Patroclus arms himself in Achilles' gear but leaves behind the great spear of ashwood from Mount Pelion which only Achilles can wield. Automedon, the charioteer, yokes the divine horses, Xanthus and Balius, sired by the West Wind, with Pedasus, a mortal horse, the third steed or tracer. Achilles arranges his army in five companies under Menesthius, Eudorus, Peisander, Phoenix and Alcimedon. He then delivers a brief hortatory address, after which he returns to his hut to make a libation from a special cup for Zeus, praying that Patroclus may win glory, yet return in safety to the ships. But Zeus will grant only one half the prayer, for Patroclus must die on the Trojan plain.

Like a swarm of wasps the Myrmidons stream, eager for battle. As the Trojans see them, supposing Achilles to have swallowed his wrath, they turn in terror. After the first spear-cast by Patroclus, each lord of the Achaeans kills his man among the fleeing Trojans. Many Trojans are cut off as they attempt to recross the trench, but Patroclus's divine horses bound over it, charging always after Hector. When Hector escapes toward Troy, Patroclus turns and mops up those caught behind him. Sarpedon, son of Zeus, at last decides to turn and stand against Patroclus.

Zeus on Olympus is deeply troubled and is tempted to save his son from the fate in store for him. But Hera sharply objects that he must not tamper with the sealed doom of a mortal. What if, moreover, the other gods should rescue their favorites. But, she suggests, let Sleep and Death convey him to his homeland, Lycia, where he may receive burial.

In the combat, Sarpedon kills Pedasus, Achilles' mortal horse, which Automedon promptly cuts loose. But Sarpedon falls to Patroclus's spear. From the ground, dying, he calls to his companion Glaucus to rally round his body, for it will be forever to Glaucus's shame if Sarpedon is despoiled by the Danaans.

Glaucus, who has a painful arrow wound in his arm, prays to Apollo to staunch the bleeding and ease his torment that he may retrieve Sarpedon's corpse. The god heeds his petition, and Glaucus urges Hector to bring the Trojans to the defense of their great Lycian ally. Patroclus encourages the Achaeans for the contest. Zeus casts darkness where the battle rages, to make more terrible the conflict over his son's body, by now barely recognizable under the gore and dust. Patroclus rages most boldly, leading his army. Zeus decides to grant Patroclus still greater honor, permitting him to rout Hector, into whose breast he sows panic. The Argives snatch Sarpedon's armor, but Zeus dispatches Apollo to bear away the body and place it in the hands of the twin brothers, Sleep and Death, to bear to Lycia.

> **COMMENT:** This close relationship between Sleep and Death, which we do not feel so strongly as the Greeks, has meaning. Life is struggle and conflict, not passive existence. We have the expression, "He is a good boy when he is asleep." For Aristotle, the great Greek philosopher, a man asleep was neither good nor bad; a man could be judged only by his actions, not by his inherent moral disposition. Sleep was thus like death for the Greeks.

Patroclus charges after the Trojans and Lycians, driving them to the wall of Ilium. Thrice he charges the citadel, and three times Apollo thrusts him back. As he attacks for the fourth time, Apollo warns him with a terrible cry: "Back! it is not your destiny to conquer the city of the Trojans." Patroclus yields.

> **COMMENT:** Note that Apollo, holding off the Achaeans, is not breaking Zeus's injunction about gods not entering the war; he is rather a symbol for destiny.

Apollo, in the guise of Asius, an uncle of Hector's, goads Hector's spirit to encounter Patroclus. Patroclus too is eager for the contest, and with a stone kills Cebriones, Hector's charioteer. Hector clings to Cebriones' head, Patroclus to his foot, as they struggle for the body, with the allies joining the fray, until at last the Achaeans prove superior. Then Patroclus, like the god of war, three times lunges against the foe, thrice bringing down nine men. The fourth time it is Phoebus Apollo who stands in his way, Apollo who taps him with his palm across his back. The armor of Patroclus falls off, and the hero is dazed. The bold Euphorbus stabs Patroclus with the spear. As he shrinks back among the Achaeans, Hector delivers the death stroke.

> **COMMENT:** Note that Hector does not slay Patroclus in an act of individual heroism, yet he will later be credited with full blame for the deed, for he is the embodiment of the united Trojan resistance to the Achaeans.

Hector taunts Patroclus, who asserts that Fate and Phoebus Apollo slew him, then Euphorbus, and only third did Hector strike. Moreover, Hector himself is soon to die at the hands of Achilles.

> **COMMENT:** The words of a dying man had prophetic content for the Greeks.

Patroclus dies, and Automedon withdraws the horses.

BOOK XVII

THE ARISTEIA OF MENELAUS

Menelaus steps forth to protect Patroclus's body, and Euphorbus challenges him for the prize, vaunting that he wil slay the son of Atreus. Menelaus, sensitive concerning his valor, boasts of how he conquered Hyperenor who had dubbed Menelaus the weakest of the Achaean nobles. In an exchange of spearcasts, Menelaus fells Euphorbus, who falls like a young tree uprooted by a gale. Apollo, in the guise of Mentes, a leader of the Cicones, draws Hector to the scene of conflict, with the news of Euphorbus's death. Menelaus, frightened by Hector's cry, and the pursuing Trojans, shrinks back from the corpse, leaving the armor for Hector to strip, and runs in search of Aias, son of Telamon, to help him rescue the body. The two kings stand over the body and Hector retreats from the huge Aias. Glaucus scolds Hector for not maintaining the effort to snatch the body of Patroclus, which might then have been exchanged for Sarpedon and his armor. Hector scowls and reminds Glaucus that courage and fear are dispensed by Zeus, who can make any man turn to flight. He then decides to put on the splendid armor of Achilles, and thus to return to do battle with the Achaeans.

Zeus looks down upon Hector, and speaks of his approaching death; for now, let him have glory, but he shall never return to the arms of Andromache, his wife. Zeus then causes Hector to fill the great armor.

Hector exhorts the chieftains of the Trojans and their allies to the conflict over Patroclus's body, offering half the spoils to the man who retrieves it. Aias, as he sees the Trojan charge, fears that the Argive defenders will be trapped away from the lines, and he urges Menelaus, famous for his war-cry, to shout for help. Aias, son of Oileus, responds, as does Idomeneus and his squire, Meriones. At first the Trojans force back the Achaean lords, but led by the resolute Telamonian Aias, most stalwart of the Argives next to Achilles, the Achaeans dash into the foe and scatter the Trojans. Hippothos, having tied his shield-strap to the ankle of Patroclus, tries to drag the body away, but he falls to the spear of Aias. A sharp exchange of spears leaves the Danaans victorious and gives them courage to charge behind the retreating Trojans, but Apollo, in the form of Periphas, the herald, rouses Aeneas, so that the Achaeans may not exceed their allotted destiny and capture Troy too soon. Aeneas recognizes the god and takes courage, shouting to the Trojans that Zeus is still on their side.

> **COMMENT:** The gods serve many functions in the *Iliad*. In their role of disguised assistants, however, it is clear that Homer is unwilling to stress their anthropomorphic intervention in human affairs. The "divine machinery" rather expresses "psychic intervention," or inspiration outside or beyond the usual faculties or capacities of a human being. Professor E. R. Dodds, in the first chapter of *The Greeks and the Irrational* (see bibliography), suggests that "the inward monition, or the sudden unaccountable feeling of power, or the sudden unaccountable loss of judgment, is the germ out of which the divine machinery developed."

The battle around the corpse of Patroclus causes the earth to run red with blood, and a thick fog lies spread over the scene of combat. Elsewhere, however, the sun shines brightly on the rest of the Achaeans and Trojans.

> **COMMENT:** Darkness is a vivid visual symbol for death which Homer frequently employs. A natural explanation, if one is desired, might be that the dust raised by the close combat shadows the sun.

All day the contest for the body drags on, with neither side yielding.

Achilles is yet in ignorance of the death of his squire.

The horses of Achilles, at a distance from the battle, stand weeping, with heads bowed to the earth, motionless, like a stele or tombstone planted on a burial mound, and Automedon, though he beats them, can not make them move.

> **COMMENT:** Herodotus, the great Greek historian, describes the ritual for the burial of Scythian kings in Book IV, chapters 71-72, of his famous *History* of the Persian War. Fifty horses are strangled and stuffed, and then mounted with bit and bridle, each with a dead youth upon it. This extravagant custom doubtless derives from a more simple procedure in which the horses of a prince served as his grave sign, and we may

suppose that Homer's picture of Achilles' horses mourning for Patroclus is borrowed from such a burial rite.

Zeus is filled with pity for the immortal horses that must suffer for mortal men, and he fills their limbs with strength so that they will not be captured by Hector. Automedon charges with the swift steeds into the fray, but, alone in the chariot, he is unable to control the chariot and employ his weapons. Alcimedon rebukes him for his folly, and together they manage the chariot. Hector, spying them, calls to Aeneas to help him catch the divine horses and chariot. Automedon calls to the Aiantes and Menelaus for help. Automedon kills Aretus, and the Aiantes come running up, compelling Hector and Aeneas to yield.

Descending in mist, Athena in the form of Phoenix exhorts Menelaus to fight valiantly for the body of Patroclus, filling him with strength and courage when he prays to her. Apollo inspires Hector, assuming the guise of Phaenops, son of Asius. Then Zeus, brandishing the aegis, lets peal a clap of thunder, giving victory to the Trojans and casting dread into the hearts of the Argives. Menelaus and Aias also become aware that Zeus is hostile to them. Aias prays Zeus that at least the fog should be lifted, and Zeus grants his wish. Menelaus, now able to see clearly, runs to find Antilochus, son of Nestor, with instructions to make haste to Achilles to tell him of Patroclus's death. Antilochus, who had not yet received the dire news, hears in horor the words of Menelaus and dashes away toward the tent of Achilles. Menelaus returns to defend the body of Patroclus.

Aias suggests that the Aiantes hold off the Trojans, while Menelaus and Meriones carry off the body, for, as Menelaus reminds him, Achilles cannot fight since his armor has been lost. Laboring hard, and continually harassed by Hector and Aeneas, the Achaean lords slowly bear the corpse toward the ships.

BOOK XVIII

THE SHIELD OF ACHILLES

Achilles, seeing the Danaans across the plain, suspects that Patroclus has been slain. At the same time Antilochus arrives with the baleful news. Achilles sinks to the ground, pours dust and ashes about his head, lying in his hugeness upon the ground. And the handmaidens of Achilles and Patroclus come out and mourn around him.

> **COMMENT:** The language describing Achilles lying in ashes resembles the language employed elsewhere in the *Iliad* to describe dead heroes. The maidens who stand around Achilles and weep for him as well as for Patroclus are comparable to the usual complement of lamenting women for a dead man. Homer thus incorporates a deliberate ambiguity into the scene, connecting Patroclus's death with the death of Achilles. That Antilochus holds Achilles' hands to prevent his suicide is adduced as reason to suspect the line was added to the original *Iliad* by someone other than Homer, since "it introduces the idea of suicide, which is elsewhere unknown in the *Iliad*" (Walter Leaf). Suicide, however, is a dominant motif in the poem; Achilles will slay Hector, who is wearing Achilles' own armor, and with the knowledge that his own death must immediately follow upon Hector's. The suggestion of suicide is clearly appropriate here.

Thetis, the mother of Achilles, hears his moan where she resides in the depths of the sea, and she wails in turn, and all the nymphs of the sea, the daughters of the sea-god Nereus, beat their breasts (an ancient gesture of lamentation) and grieve with her. The Nereids, as they are called, are enumerated in a catalogue, which begins and ends upon a similar line: "all those along the depth of the sea who were Nereids," reads the introductory verse, while the closing line runs, "and the others along the depth of the sea who were Nereids."

THE ILIAD

COMMENT: This is a species of poetic technique known as "ring composition," common in lyric forms.

Thetis keens for the sorrows her son must endure and leads the chorus of nymphs to the shore by Achilles' ships, to ask what grief has come to him. Achilles tells of Patroclus's death, how Hector wears his armor, and exclaims that he has no will to live until he has taken revenge upon the Trojan leader. Thetis then reveals that Achilles must die soon after Hector meets his fate.

Achilles replies: "Then let me perish. I have been useless to my friends, a burden on the earth. I wish that strife would vanish from among gods and men. But for now let me forget the quarrel between Agamemnon and myself, and return to wreak vengeance on Hector. If I must die, that fate awaits the best of men; I will seek my glory."

Thetis answers that Achilles cannot rescue the body or help his hard-pressed companions-in-arms without armor, but that she will visit Hephaestus, god of crafts, and beg him to prepare armor for Achilles, which she will deliver on the morrow. Till then he must refrain from the fighting.

The nymphs return to report to their father Nereus what has caused their sorrow, and Thetis departs for Olympus.

The Trojans, meanwhile, pursuing the Achaeans to the ships, once again overtake the body, and Hector threatens to take it from the Aiantes. Hera, however, sends Iris to Achilles to urge him to prepare for action. Achilles, learning that Hera has dispatched the messenger-goddess, asks her how he may enter battle without armor, repeating his mother's injunction, and recalling that no other equipment can fit him, except perhaps the great shield of Telamonian Aias, who is surely making use of it himself. Iris counsels him to go to the trench unarmed, for by his very presence he may frighten the Trojans and give the Argives the opportunity to bring in the body. Athena hangs upon his shoulders the aegis, and a blaze shines forth from his head and body like a flame in the night.

At the wall Achilles thrice utters his piercing war-cry. The Trojans fall back in fear, some dying upon their own comrades' spears in the melee. The Achaeans meanwhile draw Patroclus away from the scene of battle.

Hera than causes the sun to set, giving respite to the Achaeans. The Trojans hold a council, and too disturbed to take seats, they stand throughout, in terror at the thought that Achilles is re-entering the battle. Polydamas, son of Panthous, who alone can tell the future as well as know the past, wisely recommends that the Trojans retire into their city, now that Achilles is back, else many will perish in disorderly retreat before his slaughtering hands. Behind the walls, they can fight safely. Hector is nettled by this advice. Too long has he been confined within the citadel. Now boldly he declares his intention to meet Achilles, if necessary, but in any case the armies must decide the victory in open combat. The Trojans applaud the poor counsel of Hector, ignoring the wise words of Polydamas.

> **COMMENT:** Because Polydamas will be proved correct, Hector will forfeit his title to leadership of the Trojans as well as his life.

The Achaeans meanwhile bemoan Patroclus, led in the dirge by Achilles, who recalls the false promise he made to Menoetius, the father of Patroclus, that he would return his son in safety to Opus, his homeland, with the glory and spoils of victory. Now both, he sees, have been destined to die at Ilium. Achilles vows that he will not perform the funeral rites for Patroclus before he kills Hector. Achilles has the body of his squire cleansed.

In an interlude on Olympus, Hera defends her intervention in rousing Achilles: even a mortal protects his friends and harms his enemies.

> **COMMENT:** This code—that one should perform kindnesses for one's friends, but requite enemies with evil—was the standard ethical precept of the ancient Greeks. The Christian ideal of love thine enemy was unknown to Homeric Greece; Socrates first challenged the traditional values.

Thetis meanwhile comes to Hephaestus' brilliant palace, which the god himself had built. She finds him constructing automatic tables which move by themselves on golden wheels. Charis, the god's wife, greets Thetis and reports to her husband that the nymph comes to ask a favor. Hephaestus recalls that Thetis with the nymph Eurynome nursed him when his mother cast him out from Olympus because he was born lame, and he is eager to fulfill her wish. He puts away his tools, cleans up, and hobbles to the sea-goddess.

Thetis relates that Zeus compelled her to marry a mortal, and that her son, the noblest of mortal men, has been born to misery. She tells of the quarrel with Agamemnon, and that Patroclus has died and lost Achilles' armor. She asks the god of crafts to construct a set of gear for her son. Hephaestus gladly undertakes to make most beautiful armor, beginning with the famous shield, covered with intricate and lovely engravings. On the shield he represents the earth, the sky, the sea, the sun and the moon, and the constellations. Then he fashions two cities, the one at peace, where a wedding procession is in progress, while elsewhere, in the market-place, men are assembled to witness compensation in a murder case arbitrated by the city elders. But the other city is besieged, and the inhabitants sally forth, prepare an ambush, and subsequently engage in ferocious battle.

> **COMMENT:** Note that the Trojan War is being fought in order that the laws of marriage may be respected. Thus, men are at war to serve the customs of peace. The interweaving of war and peace seems to Homer to be a necessary part of human experience.

Also on the shield are farmers ploughing a fertile field, while in another part laborers reap the acres of a king; also portrayed are vineyards and herds of livestock and dancers. Around the shield is wrought the river Ocean, which encircles the earth.

> **COMMENT:** The entire passage on the shield of Achilles is not only one of the most beautiful, poetically, in the poem, but is also a kind of metaphor for the whole work. Just as the *Iliad* itself contains the variety and complexity of human motives, values and activities, so does the shield. But it also fills out in greater detail certain non-military aspects of the known world at that time which serve as a poignant contrast to the devastations of war which is the central focus of the work. Thus we see what the men at war are fighting for, what their peace-time lives were like, what such ordinary, non-heroic but vital occupation as farming consisted of, indeed, all the aspects of life that could not be portrayed in the *Iliad*'s war-context, but about which the heroes of the *Iliad* thought and from which Homer's similes drew their inspiration.

The fact that the shield portrays the entire known world reveals something of the epic spirit of Homer, the attempt to capture in words (or metaphorically here in metal) the entirety of human existence and the physical reality surrounding man. An interesting contrast to Homer's universality is Virgil's provincialism. In his *Aeneid*, Virgil, in imitation of Homer, gives to Aeneas a great shield with which to fight Turnus. But on Aeneas' shield, Virgil paints, not the entire known world, but the seven hills of Rome. Virgil is dominated by the glorification of Rome under the great Augustus, Homer by no one city or people, but the universe, itself.

The final significance of the shield is that it is presented as a conscious work of art, at a point which, however obvious, cannot be over-stressed. In the middle of the description of the furrows of a field, Homer pauses to say admiringly: "The artist had created a miracle." Here is Homer's equivalent of the warrior's *areté*. For it is also Homer who is describing with his winged words, under divine inspiration, this great artistic feat of the god Hephaestus. If the god could make a wonder, so, Homer implies, can a man. And Homer proves it by writing a wonder himself, not only this particular passage but the whole of the *Iliad*. Man, mortal though he may be, can match the gods, not in their personal immortal power but in creating an enduring work of art. This Homer has done, as the great Athenian writers and sculptors and architects were to continue to do centuries later.

Hephaestus also makes a breastplate, helmet and greaves (leg-guards) of tin, and gives the armor to Thetis, who bears it down from Olympus.

COMMENT: Greek art portrayed scenes in succession. At the beginning of a sculptured frieze, for example, riders might be striding beside their horses, while later on they would be seen riding their steeds. Thus developing events could be portrayed in literature (a technique called "ecphrasis"), the author's imagination often suggested details of action which pictorial arts could hardly represent.

BOOK XIX

THE PREPARATION FOR BATTLE

At dawn the next morning Thetis delivers the armor to her son, whom she finds mourning over Patroclus. She reminds him that Patroclus lies dead by the will of the gods and that he must give over his laments. Achilles is amazed at the armor, at which his Myrmidons dare not gaze for its splendor, and he is filled with passion for battle. He is assured by Thetis that the corpse of Patroclus will not decay and advised at last to make his peace with Agamemnon.

Achilles summons all the Achaeans to council.

> **COMMENT:** This is the second council called by Achilles (the first was in Book I). Councils are ordinarily arranged by the highest chieftain, Agamemnon. Calling the council is not, however, another token of Achilles' insubordination. Formally, Achilles is rejoining the community of the Achaeans. We must note, however, that Achilles does not eat with the rest of the Argives, but remains apart.

Achilles expresses sorrow over the quarrel, which benefited only the Trojans—better the girl had died than to have been the cause of such havoc to the Achaeans. He is willing to make peace among the lords and return to battle. The warriors are overjoyed, and Agamemnon must still the commotion when he begins to speak. He argues that Zeus and Destiny are responsible for the feud; for they sent Delusion (or "Folly"), the eldest daughter of Zeus, who walks over the heads of men to mislead them. Agamemnon tells how Zeus himself was once deceived by Folly (*até*), when Alcmene was about to bring forth Zeus's son Heracles. Zeus claimed that a wide-ruling king should be born that day, sprung from his blood. Hera induced him to swear assent to this prophecy, and then held back Heracles' birth, while securing the premature parturition of Eurystheus, son of Sthenelus descended from Zeus through Perseus. Eurystheus forced shameful tasks upon the beloved son of Zeus.

Zeus banished Folly from heaven, relegating her to the world of mortals. Just so, Agamemnon concludes, was he deluded. But he will make amends in rich gifts.

Achilles answers that he prefers to enter battle immediately. Odysseus suggests that the Achaeans take their fill of food and wine, so that hunger and thirst will not weaken and overcome them in battle. He bids Agamemnon bring out the gifts, and swear he has never slept with Briseis; also Odysseus suggests that kings can be more prompt to make amends when they have been the first to grow angry.

Agamemnon assents and orders that the men remain assembled until he brings out the gifts which the ambassadors had enumerated to Achilles the day before (Book IX). Achilles again announces his preference for an immediate encounter with the Trojans. But if the rest will dine, he will have nothing till he has accomplished the death of Hector.

Odysseus wisely advises that Achilles accept his bidding, since he is older and wiser. Heroes daily fall in combat; those who remain must nourish themselves.

>**COMMENT:** Here especially Achilles is disassociated from the living. Later he will be sustained on nectar and ambrosia, the food of the immortals, which is used as well in the *Iliad* to preserve the bodies of Patroclus and Hector. Note also that Achilles, unlike Hector in the previous book, yields to the counsel of the wiser man.

Odysseus dispatches lords to bring out the promised gifts: the seven tripods, twenty cauldrons, twelve horses, seven maidens, Briseis herself, and ten talents of gold. Talthybius, the herald, holds a boar which Agamemnon slays with a ritual knife, offering an oath to Zeus that he has never touched Briseis. Achilles speaks and attributes the grief of the quarrel to the will of Zeus, who plants folly in the hearts of men. The assembly is dissolved, and Myrmidons bear the gifts to Achilles' tent.

Briseis laments when she sees the body of Patroclus, for he was kind to her, and promised to make her the wife of Achilles. The other women join her in wailing, inwardly bemoaning their own hard lot. Achilles refuses all who bid him take food. He pronounces a moving speech over Patroclus, the dearest of all men to him, whose death, he asserts, has cut him more painfully than would the demise of his own young son.

Zeus takes pity on Achilles, and chides Athena for neglecting her favorite. He sends her to distil nectar and ambrosia in the veins of Achilles, that he may not feel hunger or thirst. Athena does the bidding of her father.

The men in their armor sparkle like snowflakes as they prepare for battle. Achilles, possessed by hatred for the Trojans, shines like fire in his divine gear. He takes the great spear of ash wood from Mount Pelion, which Chiron the centaur had given to his father Peleus. Automedon and Alcinous yoke the divine horses. Achilles cries to his team: "Bring back your charioteer; do not leave him dead as you did Patroclus." Then Xanthus, one of the immortal team, makes answer, for Hera puts voice into him: for now they will save Achilles, but soon he must die through no fault of theirs. Destiny wills it so, just as it was Apollo who slew Patroclus. A man and a god, they warn, will put an end to Achilles' warfare.

> **COMMENT:** This is one of the few examples of the supernatural in the *Iliad*; Homer is generally careful to remove all phenomena from his poem which contradict the laws of nature or the customs of man. Thus he substitutes the aged Phoenix for the traditional tutor of Achilles, Chiron the centaur, who is virtually excluded from the *Iliad*. Moreover, only the most oblique references suggest the tale of the sacrifice of Agamemnon's daughter, Iphigeneia. The horse's speech is thus a most startling and effective prelude to Achilles' return to battle.

Achilles retorts that he knows well his fate, yet he must give battle, nonetheless, to the Trojans. He then drives off to meet the foe.

BOOK XX

THE BATTLE OF THE GODS

Both camps prepare for battle. Zeus meantime bids Themis, goddess of order and custom, to summon the gods to council. All the rivers (except Ocean) and all the nymphs appear at the assembly. Poseidon is the first to speak, asking the reason for the council. Zeus replies that he is thinking of the impending encounter on the Trojan plain: if Achilles rages unchecked, he will swiftly destroy all resistance, contrary to destiny, and will conquer Troy. Zeus, therefore, will permit the gods to enter the combat, taking the sides of their partisans.

Instantly Hera and Athena, with Poseidon and Hephaestus, make for the Achaean ships to aid the Argives, and Ares, Phoebus Apollo, his sister Artemis, their mother Leto, and Aphrodite set off with the River Xanthus for the Trojan camp.

When the gods enter the fight, the terror of the Trojans ceases, and each side ranges aggressively against the other. Zeus thunders loudly, and Poseidon, god of earthquakes, shakes the world so fiercely that Hades, lord of the dead, fears lest the earth may crack open and the hideous abode of the dead be revealed to gods and men. Opposite each other the gods take their stand: Poseidon against Apollo, Athena against Ares, Hera against Artemis, Hermes against Leto, and Hephaestus against Xanthus the river, known among men as Scamander.

> **COMMENT:** A battle of the gods, or *theomachy*, which is an element in many mythological traditions, is here suggested to magnify the importance of the return of Achilles. The actual theomachy is postponed to the following book, where Homer employs what was very probably an ancient epic theme to express the sheer energy of war and to relate human events to cosmic struggles.

Achilles meanwhile, searches eagerly for Hector, but Apollo, taking the form of Lycaon, a son of Priam, in sarcasm addresses Aeneas, asking what has happened to the boasts he made that he would not shirk combat with the son of Peleus. Aeneas retorts that once before he encountered Achilles, when he was tending his herds on Mount Ida. Achilles sacked the towns Lyrnessus and Pedasus, and only Aeneas' swiftness of foot saved him. Athena saw to the success of Achilles that time: indeed there is always some deity to protect him. Nevertheless, Aeneas resolves to meet him. Apollo reminds Aeneas that his mother is Aphrodite, a goddess of higher rank than the sea-nymph Thetis, mother of Achilles, and that he may well expect some gods to be partial to him as well as to Achilles. Inspired with courage by Apollo, Aeneas strides against his mighty foe.

Hera meanwhile is alarmed about Achilles and bids Poseidon and Athena either to divert Aeneas or take their stand at the side of Achilles, that he may know that the most powerful gods are on the side of the Achaeans. The Trojans have only the most inconsequential immortals to protect them. Poseidon replies that there is no need for the gods to become involved in the war, but that if and when some deity sympathetic to the Trojans openly opposes the Danaans, then the partisans of the Argives would quickly reveal their superior power. Poseidon leads the gods aside to a wall built by the Trojans with the aid of Athena to protect Heracles from a monster sent by Poseidon.

> **COMMENT:** Homer subtly introduces an allusion to the construction of the Trojan wall, recalling the treachery of King Laomedon of Ilium, who earned the wrath of Poseidon by defrauding him of his rewards for building the fortification. When Heracles saved Laomedon's daughter Hesione from a sea-monster sent in vengeance by Poseidon, Laomedon cheated him as well. (This legend is told elsewhere in Greek poetry and is also reported by the *scholiasts*, ancient Greek commentators on literature, whose notes on Homer still survive in part.) The wall built by treachery is doomed to fall. We recall also the legend that Heracles sacked Troy and killed Laomedon, which suggests the coming fall of the city and, by analogy, invests with grandeur the imminent exploits of Achilles.

The gods favorable to the Danaans, covered by a thick mist, watch the battle. Their opponents take seats upon an opposite ridge.

Aeneas, meanwhile, springs forth from the multitude of the Trojans as they charge ahead against the Achaeans. Achilles leaps to the forefront of his army, and the two heroes meet. Achilles, frothing like a wounded lion, is the first to speak. He asks what has prompted Aeneas to venture out alone against him: is it the desire to be king of the Trojans? But Priam will not grant Aeneas that honor. Nor will Achilles be easy to overcome. Achilles repeats the story of Aeneas's near death at his hands on Mount Ida and warns his foe to retreat.

Aeneas retorts that he cannot be frightened as though he were a child. The noble lineage of both men, he claims, is well known— but Aeneas is willing, nevertheless, to fill in the details: Zeus was father to Dardanus, who had Erichthonius, the wealthiest man of his time, as son. Next in line was Tros (for whom Troy, obviously, was named), whose sons were Ilus (cf. Ilium), Assaracus and Ganymede whom, on account of his beauty, Zeus made immortal to be the cup-bearer of the gods. Hector is the great-grandson of Ilus, whose son was Laomedon, father of Priam. Aeneas is descended from Assaracus, father of Capys, whose son Anchises was Aeneas's own father.

> **COMMENT:** This speech seems to be a reply to Achilles' taunt about Aeneas's ambition to be king. In Book XIII there is a suggestion that Aeneas bears ill-will toward Priam. Aeneas generally is unenthusiastic about combat and must be exhorted. Note, moreover, that Achilles in his wrath is yet reluctant to engage Aeneas, and Poseidon, below, takes pity on this son of Aphrodite, though the sea-god is an implacable enemy of the Trojans. A dynastic conflict has been presumed by some scholars between Hector and Aeneas to account for these facts.

Zeus, concludes Aeneas, will grant or withhold victory. Words and insults count for nothing: the bronze spearheads must decide the issue. With that he hurls his spear, which sticks in the divine shield of Achilles, unable to pierce it.

Achilles casts in return, but Aeneas ducks and avoids the shaft. Aeneas picks up a stone which two men, says Homer, could not lift as men were in his own day, and Achilles draws his sword.

> **COMMENT:** We must note how careful Homer is not to exaggerate the powers of his heroes: the strength of two men we can easily imagine a hero to possess. Homer does not regularly endow his figures with unbelievable abilities, as epic poets in other traditions do. Virgil, for example, in Book XII of the Aeneid in a scene borrowed from the *Iliad,* grants the hero Turnus the strength of twelve men. This fact reinforces the conviction that the surrealistic battle between Achilles and

THE ILIAD

the river Xanthus is to be understood, not literally as the product of a primitive imagination, but symbolically.

Poseidon, concerned for Aeneas, who, he says, is without blame, declares his desire to protect the hero. He claims that Zeus decreed that Aeneas is to survive to continue the race of Trojans.

COMMENT: The official Roman mythology held that Aeneas was the ancestor of the Romans, presumably drawing upon this passage in the effort to link their past with the great cultural heritage of the Greeks.

Hera replies that she and Athena will save not one of the Trojans, and Poseidon must make his own decision. The god then bears Aeneas to the edge of the battle front, where the soldiers are yet arming themselves. Poseidon warns Aeneas to avoid the more powerful Achilles. When Achilles has been slain, then none of the other Achaeans will be able to harm Aeneas. Achilles, amazed that Aeneas has disappeared, turns his attention to the remainder of the Trojans, urging on the Achaeans. He reminds his men that he alone cannot hold off so numerous a horde, that they must follow him as he gives his best in combat. Hector, too, exhorts his army. Apollo admonishes Hector not to face Achilles alone.

Achilles first slays Iphition, son of Otrynteus, taunting him in bitter words. Two more he fells. Then Polydorus, the youngest son of Priam, whom Priam had forbidden to enter the war. Achilles brings him down as he runs by. Hector, enraged, stands forth to meet Achilles. As Achilles charges, Apollo wraps Hector in mist and bears him away. Thrice Achilles vainly stabs. The fourth time, like a man possessed, he lunges, hurls an acid insult at Hector, and slays many Trojans, including Tros, son of Alastor, who first seeks mercy by supplication, clutching the knees of Achilles. Like a fire Achilles rages, and his hands are covered with grime and gore.

COMMENT: Homer's similes are never arbitrary. Hector was compared to fire when he was about to ignite the Achaean ships. Here Achilles is likened to flame in anticipation of the symbolic battle between Hephaestus and Xanthus in the next book.

BOOK XXI

THE BATTLE BY THE RIVER

When the armies reach the river Xanthus, Achilles cuts off a number of the Trojans, the rest flee back to the city. The desperate Trojans leap into the stream, trying to swim in their armor against the whirling eddies. Again Achilles is likened to fire, before which locusts gather in a river.

Achilles leaves his spear on the bank and, armed only with his sword, leaps into the river to consummate the slaughter. The water runs red with blood. When he has been wearied by the killing, Achilles selects twelve young Trojans to bring back alive, whom he will sacrifice at the funeral pyre of Patroclus, as he had vowed when he learned of his squire's death. These he gives over to his fellows to conduct back to the ships.

COMMENT: Here we see one of the dire consequences of Achilles' "fatal wrath" and of his later decision to wait until Hector rages by his tent before going back to war. We saw how that decision resulted in the death of Patroclus. Now we see Achilles' response to that death in his inhuman behavior towards the twelve Trojans whom he sacrifices for the funeral of Patroclus. He commits this human sacrifice out of sheer vengeance. At this point, we observe Achilles in his most dehumanized state, overwhelmed with guilt, rage and blood-lust. He is now not only a tragic figure in that his great nobility of spirit is blemished and his heroic qualities compromised, but he is also, like a true tragic hero, in a great state of emotional anguish. In this book he will continue to act brutally even to the excess of choking the river god Xanthus, an act in which he goes beyond the moral bounds fixed for man. His final act of brutality will be his desecration of Hector's dead body. The present sacrifice of the twelve Trojans is, in many ways, the most brutal and dehumanized of his acts because he kills these victims ritually and coldly, without even the justification of the heat of the moment in battle.

THE ILIAD

Lycaon, powerless before Achilles' wrath, and finally in desperation declares that he is not from the same womb as Achilles' bitter foe, Hector.

Achilles replies that since the death of Patroclus, he cares nothing for ransom and will leave no Trojan alive, least of all the sons of Priam. "See how great I am," says Achilles, "see how beautiful! Yet I too shall die, though my mother is immortal. You also, then, resign yourself to fate."

Lycaon lets go, spreading his arms before Achilles, who slays him with his sword.

> **COMMENT:** Note Achilles' assertion that since the death of Patroclus, all kindness has been driven from his heart, thus the contrasting results of his two encounters with Lycaon.
>
> Observe also that Lycaon seems not entirely *compelled* to accept his destiny, but rather acceded to persuasion. Achilles speaks not in derision but solemnly: Achilles has chosen death by his decision to remain at Troy and slay Hector, death by the arrow of Paris, as we are reminded in the last line of his speech. Lycaon, the disarmed suppliant, can appeal to Achilles only on the grounds of their common humanity. Achilles replies to Lycaon on the same level; Lycaon releases his grip and accepts Achilles' argument.

Achilles heaves the body into the river, for the fish to feed upon, and turns upon the rest of the Trojans, vowing to slay them all to pay for the death of Patroclus and the other Achaeans who died in the absence of Achilles.

The river Xanthus, however, wants to protect the Trojans, and inspires the ambidexterous Asteropaeus, grandson of the river Axius, with courage. After a verbal exchange, Asteropaeus casts both spears, one of which draws blood from Achilles' right arm. Achilles, missing with his spear, takes the life of Asteropaeus with his sword as the latter tries for the fourth time to pull Achilles' great spear out of the river bank. Achilles shouts that he is of the blood of Zeus, through Zeacus, father of Peleus, and thus is nobler than the descendant of a river. It is Zeus, he adds, who wields the thunderbolt.

> **COMMENT:** Note that the thunderbolt again suggests **fire** versus water.

Achilles leaves the body of Asteropaeus to the eels and sets off after the Paeonians, the tribe of Asteropaeus, of whom he slays seven. But the river Xanthus speaks out angrily that already his streams are clogged with corpses and his waters are defiled through the havoc Achilles has wreaked. Let him finish his slaughter on the plain, if so Zeus has decreed. Achilles assents and hastens to his murderous task. Xanthus calls to Apollo to defend the Trojans.

Achilles leaps into the river, which surges up and spouts out all the slain, protecting the still living Trojans. Achilles is powerless against the river, and when a tree he clutches is uprooted, he dashes for the plain. The river rises in a huge wave over him, pursuing Achilles across the plain, cutting the ground out from under him. He cries out to Zeus that it was prophesied to him by his mother that Apollo was to slay him—would that Hector, he exclaims, the best of the Trojans, had won the glory of Achilles' death. That would be better than to perish so ignobly in the water.

> **COMMENT:** Since Achilles has fatalistically accepted the fact that he is to die, he seems to have transcended his own mortality. Twice he is shown his mistake: once in the death of Patroclus, whom he loves and whose mortality, therefore, catches up with Achilles; and again, here, when he sees himself subject to an ignominious death. From the time he re-enters the battle, he seems to be so nearly immortal, that we must stress Homer's reminder that Achilles, too, is only a man. Note how the gods take him by the hands like a helpless child.

Poseidon and Athena come to his aid, taking his hands and assuring him that he will survive the river. They urge him to continue his battle against the Trojans till they are penned within their citadel and he has slain Hector.

Xanthus calls to the adjacent river Simois for assistance, that together they may bury Achilles.

Hera, in fear for the hero, urges Hephaestus to his aid, bidding him scourge the plain and burn the river nor to cease before she calls him off. Hephaestus kindles first the plain, devouring the corpses in flame, then turns upon the river, consuming the foliage by its banks, singeing the fishes, and boiling the waters of Xanthus. Xanthus vainly begs him to stop and to let Achilles ravage as he will. The river then turns to Hera, renouncing all aid to the Trojans if she will check her son; the fire ceases.

> **COMMENT:** Note that the battle of the river god and the

fire god does not transgress the bounds of nature. We can conceive of a river choked with bodies rising above its banks, as well as a blaze which checks the river's flood. Conceived as a contest of antagonistic deities, however, these forces of nature emphasize the magnitude of human warfare, and focus attention on the blind energy of man which battle releases.

The combat of Xanthus and Hephaestus rouses the other deities to action, Ares, in resentment of Diomedes' spear-thrust which was guided by Athena, hitting the invincible Aegis. In return Athena drops him with a boulder in the neck, vaunting her superiority over him in combat. Hera notices that Aphrodite is leading Ares away, and sets Athena upon her. Aphrodite is stunned by a blow on the breasts. Athena boasts that Ilium should long since have fallen, if those who aid the Trojans were all like Ares and Aphrodite.

Poseidon challenges Apollo to take the first swing, since Apollo is younger. He then reminds Apollo of the time they toiled for Laomedon, when Poseidon built the wall and Apollo herded cattle, how they were defrauded of their hire, and threatened with slavery. Yet Apollo, he says, defends the people of Laomedon. Apollo refuses to engage Poseidon for the sake of mortals. Artemis, his sister, upbraids him for his retreat, and Hera, angry at her insolence, seizes her wrists and boxes her ears with her own bow. Artemis flees in tears.

Hermes declines to fight Leto, a consort of Zeus, who collects the bow and arrows of her daughter. Artemis flies up to Zeus to complain of Hera. The rest of the gods return to Olympus, but Apollo takes his stand at Troy.

Priam orders the Trojans to open the gates to their comrades to give them respite from Achilles. Apollo inspires Agenor, son of Antenor, to stand against Achilles: Agenor debates whether to run or to face the man, and concluding that Achilles will easily catch him if he flees, he prepares for the encounter. Agenor bravely announces his intention of holding off Achilles and saving the city of the Trojans, and then casts vainly with his spear, which bounds off the divinely wrought greaves of Achilles. Before Achilles can strike back, Apollo wafts Agenor away in a mist, and then, leading Achilles away from Ilium and toward the river Xanthus, permits the Trojans to return safely to their city.

BOOK XXII

THE DEATH OF HECTOR

The Trojans now are safely within the walls of Ilium, as the Achaeans approach. But Hector, bound by destiny, remains outside the town, in front of the Scaean Gates.

Phoebus Apollo meantime reveals himself to Achilles and asks why Achilles pursues a god, whom he can never catch or kill, and allows the Trojans to escape. Achilles angrily replies that he would punish the god for such treachery, if he were able. He then bolts toward the city. Priam, king of Troy, sees Achilles sweeping across the plain, looking like the star Orion's Dog (Sirius)—the brightest of the stars, but the one which brings on the season of fever, and thus a baneful star. Priam calls down to Hector in anguish to come within the citadel and not await Achilles, for to wait may mean his death. Priam notes with sorrow that the brothers Lycaon and Polydorus are not to be seen inside, and he speculates on ransom if they are not already dead. Priam at last appeals in the name of the city, the women and children of Troy, that Hector take pity and preserve himself.

> **COMMENT:** Hector, it should be observed, has not proved very successful in single combat; he cannot stand up to Achilles, Aias or Diomedes, for example. His role is not that of the individual champion, seeking personal glory, but rather he is seen always as the defender of Ilium, very frequently in the context of women or children. Hector, the hero of family and tribe, should retreat to save himself for his people; his fate, however, impels him to the suicidal encounter.

Priam cries that he himself will be slain by the invaders and cast to the dogs. A young man, he says, looks handsome in death, but there is nothing more unsightly than an aged man lying mutilated in the dust. Priam tears his hair, but Hector is unmoved.

Hecabe, then, his mother, holds forth her breast to remind Hector that she nursed him and begs him not to permit himself to die outside the city, where the Achaeans will take him and feed his body to the dogs. Hector, however, waits like a poisonous snake in the mountains, furious against Achilles.

Hector debates with himself his course of action. If he returns to the citadel, Polydamas will reproach him for sacrificing so many Trojans, since Hector did not heed the advice to turn back in the night to the walls of Ilium. Better, he says, to take his chances with Achilles, than endure this certain shame.

> **COMMENT:** Note that Hector is ashamed, not because he lacked courage—in fact he was too bold—but because he recklessly put his people in danger. Compare this with Achilles, who wrathfully jeopardized the entire Achaean army by his withdrawal from the fight.

Hector wonders whether he can put off his armor and approach Achilles in peace, promising the return of Helen plus all the wealth that lies in Ilium. But he realizes that Achilles might well kill him naked, as if he were a woman: there is no way for Hector to converse with Achilles like boy and girl. It must be battle.

As Achilles approaches, Hector no longer is able to face him, but turns and runs, with Achilles in quick pursuit like a hawk on the tail of a dove. Achilles keeps Hector away from the wall and the Trojan allies, and the two run to a pair of springs that flow from the river Scamander. One spring constantly gives forth steaming water, while the other is cold as ice in all seasons. By these streams the Trojan women in former times washed their clothes, before the war befell them. Here Hector and Achilles race faster than contesting runners, for the prize is Hector's life.

The gods survey the chase, and Zeus, recalling the piety of Hector, debates whether to rescue him from his fate. Athena retorts that the other gods will not approve if Zeus breaks the bonds of destiny and saves a mortal from his appointed doom. Zeus replies that he does not mean to offend her. He will let her do her will.

> **COMMENT:** Homer imparts human will to the guardians of destiny, while binding them by the firm laws of fate. Thus destiny is at once blind and full of meaning. The student should examine this paradox—that is, this seeming contradiction—throughout the poem: all the subjective impressions of meaningless death and destruction which are recorded in the *Iliad*, in the context of the unfolding "will (or plan) of Zeus" (cf. Book I, 1. 5).

Achilles follows like a dog after a fawn, Hector trying to get near Ilium that the men on the wall might protect him with their spears and javelins, while Achilles constantly cuts him off and drives him into the plain. As in a dream they run, the one pursuing but unable to catch up, the other fleeing yet incapable of escaping. Achilles shakes his head at his men so that they will not hurl spears at Hector and rob him of the honor.

Then Zeus weighs portions of death in his golden scales; the lot of Hector is heavier and tilts downward. Apollo, who has given strength and speed to Hector abandons him, whereas Athena stands beside Achilles, assuring him of victory.

Athena, likening herself to Hector's brother, Deiphobus, comes up to Hector and urges that together they turn and face Achilles. Hector is filled with love and gratitude toward his brother, who alone, he imagines, has dared to step forth and assist him. Athena lies, saying that Priam and Hecabe tried to interfere, but could not avail. Hector now announces to Achilles that he will cease his flight, having run three times around the city of Troy. He promises not to defile Achilles' body, but to return it stripped to the Achaeans, and begs Achilles to do the same. Achilles bitterly replies that just as there can be no agreement between men and lions, or sheep and wolves, so there can be no friendship between Hector and Achilles. Let Hector be brave, his death is near. With that Achilles cast his spear, which Hector ducks under and avoids; but Athena retrieves it and returns it to Achilles. Hector boasts that Achilles will not stab him in the back like a coward, and suggests that the gods may yet grant him the victory—Achilles' death would relieve the hard-pressed Trojans. Hector's spear strikes Achilles' divine shield but bounces off. Hector turns to Deiphobus and calls for another spear, but his brother is nowhere to be seen. Then Hector realizes the treachery of Athena and says aloud that Zeus has decided his death. Yet he will die courageously, with a final act of valor.

COMMENT: Coming in a mist, Athena helps to destroy this most human of heroes. The scene is classic in its presentation of the way symbol and psychology interact, as they do so often in Homer. For, in a naturalistic sense, we may say that Hector so desired and needed help to fight Achilles that he literally "sees" Deiphobus. It is a kind of hallucinatory wish-fulfillment. Hector—and Homer—knows that the ceaseless run around the walls of Troy cannot go on. Something must break into that circle. Time, the story, the destiny of Achilles cannot be foiled. Both heroes know this for themselves. In addition, Hector has his pride and knows that he cannot keep running lest he shame

THE ILIAD

himself. The will of Zeus will out, and the moment the entire poem has been leading up to dramatically must be consummated. But, in this battle, it is not only Hector's life which is at stake, for the death of Hector also presages the death of Troy.

Theologically, the scene makes another one of Homer's indirect stabs at the terrible relationship between men and the gods. It would appear that the gods exist essentially to deceive men, to make them see what is not. To the end, they make Hector think he will win, when all know he must die.

Like an eagle Hector charges with drawn sword. But Achilles is protected by his armor, and his spear point glistens like the evening star as he scans Hector's armor for a vulnerable spot. Spying the open space around the throat above the breastplate, Achilles thrusts and brings down Hector. He mocks the pride of Hector, who slew Patroclus but forgot the great avenger who remained alive. Now the dogs and carrion birds will feed on Hector's corpse. Hector with his dying breath begs Achilles to accept ransom and return his body to the Trojans for cremation and burial, but Achilles savagely retorts that his prayers are worthless. Achilles would cut the meat off Hector and eat it raw if he could, nor would he return the corpse for its weight in gold. His parents shall not mourn Hector on his death-bed.

COMMENT: Achilles' cannibalistic threats may also be associated with certain primitive death rites, in which the body of the deceased was consumed by his kin; cf. Herodotus, the Greek historian, Book III, ch. 38, for example.

Hector sees that Achilles' heart is iron and warns him to beware the curse of the dying man. He predicts that Paris and Apollo will slay Achilles. His soul departs for Hades, lamenting its destiny. Achilles tells the corpse that he will accept his own death when it is appointed, and he withdraws his spear from the body and strips it of armor—his armor. The rest of the Achaeans rush forth and every one stabs the body of great Hector.

Achilles is tempted to try the rest of the Trojans, but he recalls Patroclus, whom, he claims, he will remember even in Hades, and he leads the men back to the ships, exulting in the glory of Hector's death.

Achilles fastens thongs through holes pierced in Hector's ankles, and ties the corpse to his chariot so that the head hangs behind in the dust. Then, whipping up his team, he drags the body across the plain, defiling the young hero. Hector's parents, observing the desecration from the wall, wail and tear their hair, while the Trojans and their allies lament as though the city were being destroyed. Priam tries to leave Ilium to beg Achilles in the name of his old father, Peleus, so that Achilles may take pity and return Hector, whose loss grieves Priam more than the loss of all the other sons who have fallen to Achilles. Hecabe leads the women of Troy in the dirge, moaning that her son who was loved and worshipped as a god has been destroyed.

Andromache, Hector's wife, summons a bath for Hector in her house, for she is still in ignorance of his fate. When she hears the mourning from the wall, she suspects the truth, and races madly to the edge of the city, where she sees Hector being dragged toward the beach. She swoons. When she revives, she cries that she and Hector share one fate. She is left a widow, their son Astyanax without a protector—he will thus be ill-treated by his playmates and will mature beneath the scorn of his companions. Hector now lies dead and naked, though there is clothing enough at home. Yet that she will burn, for there is no use for the garments. The women of Troy mourn with her.

BOOK XXIII

THE FUNERAL GAMES

The Trojans mourn Hector, but the Achaeans disperse to their own ships—all except the Myrmidons, who are ordered by Achilles to draw up with their chariots around the body of Patroclus. When they have lamented the dead hero, they may disarm, clean themselves and dine. Achilles leads the dirge, and the sand grows wet with tears as the Myrmidons proceed thrice around the body. Achilles reiterates his promise to throw Hector to the dogs and consign twelve Trojan youths to the flames with the body of Patroclus. The Myrmidons unyoke their horses, remove their arms, and partake of the funeral feast.

The Achaean lords lead Achilles to Agamemnon and try to persuade Achilles to bathe, but he refuses till the pyre for Patroclus has consumed the body, and he bids Agamemnon to give orders to collect wood. Then the Danaans can return to their tasks.

Agamemnon consents; they all feast and turn to their tents for sleep, except Achilles who lies moaning on the shore, among his men, until he too succumbs to weariness. In his sleep the ghost of Patroclus visits him, standing above his head. The shade speaks: Let Achilles bury his companion forthwith, that he may cross the river to Hades' house and join the souls of the dead. No more then shall he return to the sight of the living, for destiny has dragged him from the company of Achilles. Patroclus foretells the death of Achilles at Troy, and begs that their bones may lie in the same golden urn, which Thetis gave to her son, for they grew up as inseparable friends, after Menoetius led him to the house of Peleus because Patroclus had accidentally killed another child in play.

Achilles replies that he is fulfilling all of Patroclus's requests, and tries to embrace the ghost. The spirit disappears, and Achilles awakes in wonder that the soul survives in Hades, though with no real life or substance.

108   THE ILIAD

COMMENT: This passage is of interest to anthropologists, some of whom find in dreams the source of belief in ghosts and afterlife.

In the morning Agamemnon sends out the men to collect timber, under Meriones, the squire of Idomeneus. They pile the wood before Achilles on the beach, and sit down. The Myrmidons in armor in their chariots convey the body of Patroclus to the cremation pile. It is covered with locks of their hair, cut off as a token of sorrow. Achilles cuts off a lock grown long as an offering to the river Spercheus, consecrating it instead to Patroclus.

Agamemnon orders a limit to the mourning—in all things there is a proper measure—and the men disperse for dinner. Those closest to Patroclus build the pyre, skin animals, and wrap the body in fat. Achilles slays four horses, two dogs belonging to Patroclus, and the twelve Trojans, adding them to the flames, vowing to defile the body of Hector and feed it to the wild beasts. Aphrodite, however, protects the body of Hector, keeping the dogs away and preventing any decay or lacerations.

When the pyre does not light, Achilles prays to Boreas and Zephyrus, the north and west winds. Iris delivers his prayers to the home of the winds, who leave their feast and roar over the Trojan plain, raising a great blaze all night, while Achilles wails like a father over a dead son.

Achilles falls asleep at dawn and is soon awakened by the Achaean kings, whom he bids put out the flames with wine and collect the bones of Patroclus. They obey and build a slight mound for him, awaiting the day when Achilles will join him to build a great one for the two heroes. Achilles then prepares the funeral games.

The first contest is the chariot race, with a servant-woman and a tripod as first prize; a mare heavy with a mule as second; a cauldron as third; gold as the fourth; and a jug as last prize. He says that his own horses would surely win were they to compete, but they mourn for their driver and will not race. Eumelus, son of Admetus, stands forth, then Diomedes with Aeneas's horses; next Menelaus with Aethe, his brother's steed, and Podargus. Then Antilochus stands up, and his father Nestor delivers a long speech of advice, stressing the fact that skill is more important than fast horses. He suggests that Antilochus hug the turning post without actually touching, for that is the most crucial maneuver. Meriones is the fifth contestant. The contestants draw lots for their lanes. Achilles stations Phoenix at the turning post. At the crack of the whip, the chariots fly. Eumelus takes the lead, followed closely by Diomedes, but Apollo causes the son of Tydeus to lose his whip, and he lags behind. Athena returns the whip to Diomedes, and enraged she breaks the yoke of Eumelus's chariot, sending him sprawling and bruised on the ground. Antilochus rides a close fourth behind Menelaus, threatening his horses with slaughter if they slacken. Antilochus runs neck and neck with Menelaus as they approach a narrow portion of the road, disregarding Menelaus's warnings, until the latter yields to prevent a collision.

Idomeneus sees Diomedes in the lead and announces that some mishap must have befallen Eumelus. Aias, son of Oileus, a partisan of Emelus, berates Idomeneus for empty talk. Achilles intervenes to stop the quarrel.

> **COMMENT:** Aias, son of Oileus, is endowed with an unpleasant and insolent character, which directly causes his death according to Book IV, 1. 502, of the *Odyssey*, where, as Proteus relates to Menelaus, Aias claims to have escaped a storm despite the gods, rather than with their aid. Another Greek epic poem described Aias's dragging Cassandra, daughter of Priam, away as she clutched the Palladium, a statue of Pallas Athena. Some legends report that he raped Cassandra. Below, he perhaps receives proleptic (i.e. anticipatory) retribution.

Diomedes comes in well ahead of the competitors, followed by Antilochus with Menelaus close after, having caught up again by virtue of his swifter horses; then comes Meriones, with Eumelus last. Achilles takes pity on Eumelus, offering him second prize as consolation, but Antilochus objects, arguing that Achilles can give other gifts to Eumelus, but the mare is his. Achilles agrees, but Menelaus, angry with Antilochus, rises to claim the horse for himself, challenging Antilochus to take an oath that he employed no treachery in gaining his victory. Antilochus wisely and modestly excuses his misconduct on the grounds of youthful impetuosity and yields the mare wtih the promise of other gifts to the superior age and stature of Menelaus. Menelaus, too, is softened, and with a warning about further indiscretions, gives up the mare to the noble youth who has endured much for his sake in the war.

> **COMMENT:** The funeral games provide a striking contrast to the rest of the *Iliad*. Here the contests are supervised fairly, most serenely, by Achilles. Arguments are mediated by reason; each man gains a fitting prize without rancor. The dispute between Menelaus and Antilochus is, in a sense, a peaceful reflection of the quarrel between Agamemnon and Achilles which

motivates the poem. While Achilles would not yield his prize to the age and rank of the commander-in-chief of the Argives, Antilochus bows with respect before precisely these qualities in the brother of Agamemnon. And while Agamemnon persisted in his folly, here Menelaus displays a proper regal detachment and pardons the transgression of Antilochus. It must be noted that this reigning peace obtains in the context of funeral games, and anticipates the almost death-like scene of reconciliation between Priam and Achilles which will be effected in the next book. The mark of life is conflict in the *Iliad*.

Meriones takes fourth prize, and Achilles presents the fifth to old Nestor, who accepts with a speech reminiscing on his former feats. As a lad, in the funeral games for King Amarynceus, he bore off all the prizes save the charioteer's, but now old age prevents him from competing. In gladness he wishes well to the noble Achilles.

Next is the boxing contest. Epeius, son of Panopeus, claims the mule, the victor's prize, asserting that he may be inferior in battle, but in boxing, his opponent must be content with second place. Only Eurylaus accepts the challenge. Diomedes helps him don the leather straps for his hands. Epeius drops Eurylaus with a solid blow to the cheek and helps him to his feet, and his companions bear him out.

Aias, son of Telamon, and Odysseus rise for the wrestling contest. Neither can budge the other. At last Odysseus with superior skill, hooks his leg behind Aias's knee as Aias lifts him in the air and brings down his opponent. He apparently also conquers in the second fall, but Achilles interrupts the battle before the third fall can begin, offering equal gifts to the two contestants

COMMENT: Aias's defeat may again be a proleptic suggestion of the contest for the arms of Achilles, where Odysseus is granted the armor of the dead hero and Aias commits suicide in his rage at the alleged treachery of Achilles. The contest is peacefully resolved, like Menelaus's argument with Antilochus. (Some think that Odysseus and Aias draw in the contest—cf. H. J. Rose in the Oxford Classical Dictionary, s.v. Aias—but the present interpretation, following Walter Leaf, enhances the meaning of the poem.)

In the footrace which follows, Aias, son of Oileus, Odysseus, and the young Antilochus compete. Aias takes an early lead, but Odysseus pressed hard upon him. He offers a prayer to Pallas Athena, who trips up Aias near the end of the race in a pile of dung, so that Odysseus comes in first (see Commentary note above on Aias). Antilochus arrives last, praising the elder Aias and the still more aged Odysseus, who comes from an earlier generation of men. A kind word for Achilles gains him an extra half-talent of gold.

The armor of Sarpedon and the sword of the slain Asteropaeus are the prizes for the armed combat game, the latter award for the winner, the former to be held equally by both contestants. Telamonian Aias and Diomedes fight, and after a vain thrust from Aias, the Achaeans halt the combat in fear for Aias, and Diomedes is presented with the sword.

A lump of precious iron is the prize for the man who throws it farthest. Epeius makes a slight cast; Leonteus surpasses him, and Telamonian Aias beats the preceding two, but Polypoetes heaves it far beyond all the others.

Ten double-bladed and ten single-bladed axes go to the contestants in the archery contest, who must aim to hit a dove tied to the mast of a ship. Teucer fires without a prayer to Apollo and misses the bird, but severs the string, for which the single axes are the reward. Meriones swiftly grabs the bow, and with a vow to Apollo, fires and brings down the fleeing dove.

Agamemnon and Meriones rise to enter in the spear-throwing competition, but Achilles, in deference to Agamemnon, presents him with first prize without a contest, and Meriones is content with the consolation award.

BOOK XXIV

THE RANSOMING OF HECTOR

The Achaeans return to their ships to dine and sleep, but Achilles still mourns for Patroclus, recalling all the hard experiences they had shared. He lies awake till dawn, weeping, pacing the beach, dragging the body of Hector thrice around the tomb—but Apollo protects it from defilement.

Many of the gods take pity on Hector, but not Poseidon or Athena or Hera, who remember the judgment of Paris, who awarded the prize for beauty to Aphrodite in return for which he was granted Helen to wed, thus causing the great war. Apollo, however, defends the pious Hector, berating the immortals for their unyielding hatred, and condemning the pitiless Achilles, who is without shame before mankind. A man must lose still dearer companions than Achilles has, but there is a limit to sorrow. Achilles offends the gods with his wrath.

Hera replies that Achilles is the son of a goddess, and therefore deserves more honor and pride than Hector.

Zeus decides that even though Achilles is greater than Hector, Hector, too, deserves mercy. It is unwise, however, to send Hermes to steal the body, for Thetis keeps watch. Rather he will ask her to persuade Achilles to accept the ransom of Priam for the body. Iris drops to the sea's bottom to find Thetis in mourning for her son so soon to die and summons her to Olympus. Thetis consents, and they fly to the seat of the gods. Zeus relates the dispute which for nine days has been current among the deities. Should Hermes Argeiphontes steal Hector's body or should Achilles still be honored? He concludes that Thetis should warn Achilles that Zeus is not pleased at his too great dudgeon. He will send Iris to Priam, suggesting that Priam bear ransom, if Achilles can be moved.

Thetis speeds to earth and sits by Achilles, urging him to eat, sleep, lie in love, and end his mourning. Already his destiny is upon him, and Zeus more than all the other gods is angry at his treatment of Hector. Achilles should accept ransom.

> **COMMENT:** Zeus argues that Achilles, as a mortal, must submit to objective necessity—that is, he must eat, sleep, love, give over his laments—and not allow his subjective passions to dominate too long his functioning in the real world.

Achilles assents to the will of Zeus. Zeus then dispatches Iris to Priam to instruct him to bear gifts to Achilles, alone, with but one herald to help convey the body. Hermes will escort Priam through the Argive camp, and Achilles will take pity on the old king, for he is kind at heart and wise, and Priam will be safe. Iris finds Priam rolling in dung, with the whole city in lamentation, and she delivers her message.

Priam consults his wife Hecabe for her opinion, revealing the order from Zeus. Hecabe in horror warns him not to approach the merciless Achilles, who may slap an aged suppliant. Let them both remain safely in the palace. She would gladly devour the liver of Achilles if she could, so bitterly does she hate the man who has slain her sons. Priam replies that he will obey the god-sent messenger. He draws from his treasure chests elaborate gifts: twelve robes with mantles; twelve blankets and cloaks with an equal number of tunics; ten talents of gold, two tripods, four cauldrons, and a lovely chalice. As he leaves, he scolds the Trojans he encounters, saying that the best of lords has perished and that he would now descend to Hades as soon as possible. His nine remaining sons he also chides, accusing them of frivolity, cowardice and dishonesty, for the noble princes have all been slain. He orders them to harness his mule wagon; they obey and load it with the presents for Achilles.

Hecabe begs Priam to pray to Zeus for an auspicious omen, to see whether the god is indeed favorable to the venture. Priam consents, and having washed his hands, he pours a libation of wine and petitions Zeus for a sign. The god sends down a huge eagle flying on the right hand, which soars above the city, and the people take heart.

Idaeus, the herald, leads the mule team, and Priam rides in a chariot through the city, lamented as though he were going to his death. As Priam leaves the city and the people behind, Zeus takes pity on them and bids his son Hermes escort the aged king, so that none of the Achaeans might see him till he has reached the shelter of Achilles. Hermes ties on his golden sandals in which he soars above land and ocean and takes up the wand with which he can charm or bewitch the eyes of men, or wake those in slumber.

> **COMMENT:** In classical mythology Hermes had, besides the function of guide, the role of *psychopomp*, literally "the escorter of souls." Hermes led the spirits of the dead to the underworld. To this function his magic wand is most appropriate, and in Book XXIV of the *Odyssey* he takes up the wand to lead the souls of the slain suitors to Hades. (Leaf comments, "The whole of this passage, with the employment of Hermes, as messenger, is thoroughly Odyssean." Priam, we recall, has expressed his wish to follow Hector to Hades, and he is mourned as though dead when he leaves Ilium. His guide is the *psychopomp*, and he is invisible to the Danaans. Thus the whole atmosphere is that of death, an impression which will be reinforced in the meeting with Achilles.

At Troy, Hermes assumes the form of a young noble and encounters the pair as they pass the tomb of Ilus, where they water their animals in the river. Idaeus is terrified at the sight of the approaching stranger and sends fear coursing through the limbs of Priam, but the gentle god dispels their fright. It is dangerous, he says, for an aged man to conduct treasures in a hostile camp, but he will guide and protect Priam. Priam sees the youth as an omen of god's will, and Hermes asks whether Priam is removing his treasure for safekeeping or abandoning the city altogether now that Hector is dead. He identifies himself as a Myrmidon, and Priam then inquires of the state of his son's body. Hermes replies that he had lain twelve days but has in no way decayed or been marred, though Achilles drags him round the burial mound of Patroclus. Thus the immortals love Hector.

Priam offers the youth his chalice that he may guide him, but Hermes will accept nothing at Achilles' expense, and joining Priam in the chariot, escorts the king through the Argive camp. He casts sleep on the guards and unbolts all doors and gates, including the entrance to Achilles' hut, which is barred by a pine shaft which three men must move, except for Achilles, who alone can handle it. Then Hermes reveals his identity and bids Priam enter and entreat Achilles.

Priam goes within, leaving Idaeus outside, to find Achilles alone save for two squires, Automedon and Alcimus, who have just completed dinner. Priam embraces the knees of Achilles and kisses his hands. Achilles looks in wonder as at a fellow in exile for manslaughter. Priam breaks the silence, begging Achilles in the name of his old father to take pity on an aged man who has no further hope of seeing his beloved son alive. Many sons has Priam lost, and latest the noblest of these. Let Achilles honor the gods and have mercy on Priam, who has suffered beyond all others: he has kissed the hands of the man who has slain his sons.

Achilles is moved, weeping now for his father, now for Patroclus, while Priam at his feet mourns Hector. Compassionately Achilles raises Priam to his feet, admiring his courage in coming before the fierce hero of the Achaeans. Let both of them give over their sorrowing. For the gods wove it into the fates of men that men must live in grief, but they themselves are ever without cares. There are two urns, he says, by the door of Zeus, one of evils, the other full of blessings, and sometimes he mixes the portions, though at other times he gives a man only from the jar of evils. Peleus, his own father, was rich and noble, and was granted a goddess to wife, but he had but a single son, born to an early death and to be a grief to his father and to the Trojan people. So, too, Priam has fallen from ineffable wealth and power. But let there be an end to mourning.

Priam wishes first to set eyes on Hector, and he rouses the ire of Achilles. He knows that Priam came with the aid of the gods, he says, else he would not have had the spirit for so dangerous a task; let him not provoke Achilles to offend the immortals by doing violence to Priam. Then Automedon and Alcimus bring in the herald, Idaeus, and the ransom gifts, and Achilles bids his servant-girls cleanse the body, that Priam might not act rashly in his anger at the mutilated corpse and move Achilles to murder him. Achilles himself places the body on a bier, and with his friends lays it on the wagon, leaving two cloaks and a tunic as a shroud.

Achilles addresses the dead Patroclus, begging that he be not angry, for the ransom he has accepted is worthy, and Patroclus will get a fair share of it.

> **COMMENT:** Note that the *Iliad* opens with an unsuccessful effort at ransom: Agamemnon does not accept Chryses' gifts in exchange for the priest's daughter, Chryseis. Midway in the poem (Book IX) Achilles refuses elaborate presents rather than return to battle and forgive Agamemnon. The poem ends, however, with a successful ransom: Achilles has learned that for mortals there are no absolutes, that men must relent before a proper recompense. It is in these terms that he explains his action to the ghost of Patroclus.

But Achilles' "education" does not stop here. With his statement that "men are wretched things, and the gods, who have no cares themselves, have woven sorrow into the very pattern of our lives," he comes to a genuinely tragic vision of life. He becomes a full tragic hero in achieving what Aristotle is later to call an *anagnoresis,* a recognition or illumination about the nature of reality, human conduct and oneself. By giving up the body of Hector and submitting to forces greater than himself, Achilles crushes his pride and achieves a philosophic humility. Most important, Achilles has become "human" again, that is, he has regained what he completely lost after the death of Patroclus, his capacity for compassion. Moreover, what brought his dormant pity into operation once more was not simply the sight of Priam clutching his knees, though this is surely one of the most moving scenes in all literature. It was also Achilles' projection of the effect of his own death upon his father, Peleus. Up to this point, death has been a brutal fact of war whose only value lay in the fact that men tried to transcend it by dying gloriously. More often than not, the fear of death turned men into savages who tried to save their own lives at any cost. But now death works to another effect. It enables Achilles to see life in its true perspective. This causes him to place an emotional value on life which, in turn, produces a genuine sense of mourning at the thought of his own death. Experiencing the meaning of his own loss, he is able to feel an empathy for his enemy Hector and true pity for both their fathers. But, in the process, he also attains a firm stoic position: "You must endure and not be broken-hearted," he tells Priam, because "lamenting for your son will do no good at all. You will be dead yourself before you bring him back to life."

There is a strong implication, finally, that by submitting to the gods and giving back the body of Hector, Achilles has transcended his once fanatically held honor code. In the beginning of the *Iliad,* the taking away of the prize of a mere slave girl had caused him to alienate himself from his whole society; now he gives up his greatest prize, Hector, himself. In his earlier limited view of external honor, he had actually dishonored himself in the very act of trying to prove his honor when, as he recognized, he had only proved a "broken reed" to his companions. Now he recognizes that the external honor he would receive from being called the conqueror of the greatest Trojan warrior is relatively nothing in contrast to the real values of life: compassion, self-knowledge, humility, understanding. Having achieved a degree of these great qualities, Achilles can now face his *moira* spiritually cleansed. The process by which he rises to what might be called a higher sense of honor, though it now has little to do with glory, fully begins when he gains control of his grief for Patroclus and then asks Priam to eat with him.

Even Niobe, he relates, partook of food, after she had vaunted over Leto that the goddess had but two children, Apollo and Artemis, while she had six sons and six daughters. The divine archers slew her children who lay unburied for nine days (for the people were turned to stone), but on the tenth the gods buried them. Nevertheless, Niobe ate when worn with weeping. She still weeps, now turned into a rock. So let them now dine.

When they have eaten, Priam asks for a bed to sleep on, for he has neither eaten nor shut his eyes since Hector's death. Achilles had a bed laid outside the tent, lest one of the Achaeans should see Priam and hold up the delivery of Hector's body. He asks how much time Priam would like for Hector's burial. Priam requests that nine days be given them for lamentation, the tenth for burial and the funeral feast. On the eleventh day they would build a barrow, and the twelfth day the armies may return to battle. Achilles consents and leads the aged Trojan outside. He lies with Briseis within.

Hermes, concerned for Priam, stands over the king and bids him take fear, lest he himself be held for ransom by the Achaeans. Hermes leads Priam and his herald back to Xanthus. Cassandra is the first to spy them and announces their return. All the people rush out wailing. Priam leads the body into the palace, and Andromache leads the threnody over Hector. She foresees the capture of the city and the women led into slavery. She sees her son Astyanax cast from a tower to the plain in revenge for his father's marauding. She sorrows that no last word could she receive from Hector, for he died far from her. Then Hecabe, Hector's mother, mourns her son whom the gods have protected even in death. Lastly, Helen leads the funeral chant, recalling that never did Hector insult her, though she had brought such grief to the Trojan people. Priam announces the truce to the Trojans, and the people fulfill the burial rites. Thus ends the *Iliad*.

MAJOR CHARACTERS AND DEITIES

ACHAEANS: The term Achaean, Argive and Danaan seem synonymous in the *Iliad* and are all names for the Greeks (the words Greeks, Greece, etc., are from the Latin, the Greeks' own name for their country being Hellas).

ACHILLES: Son of Peleus and the sea nymph Thetis, leader of the Myrmidons. He is the most powerful and handsome hero in the war, characterized by a violent and headstrong individualism which produces his self-imposed excommunication from the army of the Achaeans. His wrath is the dominant theme of the *Iliad*, directed first against Agamemnon, and then, after the death of Patroclus, against Hector. In Book XXIV, in a scene which takes place in the dead of night, and through various symbolic details suggests death, Achilles becomes reconciled with his foe, Priam. Achilles' death is frequently predicted in the *Iliad;* shortly after the end of the poem he will be slain by Paris with an arrow.

Achilles is the Greek hero *par excellence;* this is the most important fact about him in the poem. He represents all the virtues and even flaws of a man of "awesome *areté.*" Indeed, Achilles is more than human; he is a demi-god in his abilities, human only in his mortality. Achilles' follows a true tragic pattern during the war. Defending his honor, he goes on to commit sins in the name of that honor, sins which both bring him to a philosophically despairing vision of life (Bk. IX), and force him into a guilty self degradation as a result of his role in causing Patroclus' death. Finally, like a true tragic hero, Achilles purges himself of his sins as he confronts the adamant forces of nature and the gods. There is a catharsis in his meeting with Priam which spiritually cleanses him and gives him back a newer, truer stature than he ever had before. Psychologically speaking, we may say that Achilles is a compulsive type of man with great sensitivity of soul combined with an overwhelmingly exalted conception of his place in society. The conflict of these two qualities provides for his great wrath, since his sensitivity makes him "over-react" to his conception of himself. Ultimately, his sensitivity and compassion triumph, but at the cost of great suffering.

THE ILIAD

AENEAS: Son of Anchises and Aphrodite, the goddess of love, and second prince of the Trojans. He is brave but generally reluctant to engage in battle, and disaffection toward the line of Priam is suggested. Perhaps a dynastic conflict with Hector explains his restrained valor.

AGAMEMNON: Son of Atreus, king of Mycenae, and commander-in-chief of the entire Achaean army. Agamemnon is lord of the largest and wealthiest realm, and hence has supreme authority. He is irresolute and quick to despair; his counsel is frequently foolish, and more than once he is sharply reprimanded by Odysseus for bad generalship. His supremacy is challenged by the younger and braver Achilles, who rejects the traditional codes of duty and respect. Agamemnon is slain by his wife, Clytemnestra, and his cousin, Aegisthus, when he returns from Troy.

AIAS: (Ajax) Son of Oileus, king of the Locrians. He is fleet of foot, bold and insolent, endowed with an unpleasant character. In the funeral games for Patroclus, he is made to slip in dung. After the action the *Iliad* covers, he is said to have raped Cassandra while she clung to the Palladium, a sacred statue of Athena at Ilium. He is subsequently drowned by Poseidon for blasphemy, as he travels home from Troy (see *Odyssey*, Book IV).

AIAS: (Ajax) Son of Telamon, king of Salamis. He is the hugest of the Achaeans and most lordly in appearance save for Achilles. His standard epithet is "bulwark of the Acheans," and he is characterized by stubborn endurance and unshakable courage, yet he is rather slow in wits, relying generally on brute strength. After the death of Achilles, he kills himself when he loses a contest with Odysseus for the armor of the slain hero.

ALEXANDER: See PARIS.

ANDROMACHE: Wife of Hector, daughter of Eetion. She is entirely devoted to Hector, whom she describes as father, mother, brother and husband to her. Andromache is the representative of wifeliness. Note that Hector is fighting for his wife, yet he is fighting on the side of Paris, who has defiled a wife and has broken the law of the hearth. Part of the tragedy of Hector and Andromache resides in this ironic circumstance. In vain she warns him to fight cautiously beneath the Trojan wall. After the fall of Troy, she is caried off by Neoptolemus, son of Achilles, who takes her as his wife.

ANTENOR: A gentle and wise Trojan, who advises the return of Helen to the Achaeans to end the war.

ANTILOCHUS: Young son of Nestor, noble but somewhat rash. By reckless driving he defrauds Menelaus of second place in the chariot race in the funeral games, but his modesty and good sense prevent exacerbation of the dispute.

APHRODITE: Daughter of Zeus and Dione, goddess of love. She is an awesome goddess in the field of love (Book III) but weak and effeminate in battle, and is wounded by Diomedes with the aid of Athena. Recall that her power is responsible for the war.

APOLLO: Son of Zeus and Leto, god of prophecy and poetry, and associated with death by disease (plague) for men, which is presumably induced by his arrows. He is represented as the defender of the walls of Troy. There is some suggestion that he is an Asian deity, perhaps connected with Lycia, a nation allied with Troy.

ARES: Son of Zeus and Hera, god of war. Homer makes him blustering, unpleasant and relatively feeble; thus he is scorned by Zeus and defeated easily by Athena. He is partial to the Trojans.

ARGIVES: See ACHAEANS.

ARTEMIS: Daughter of Zeus and Leto, sister of Apollo, goddess of the hunt and wild animals. She is associated with death by disease for women, and fights on the Trojan side.

ATE: Daughter of Zeus, the goddess or representation of Folly or Delusion. Ate is said to take possession of a man (or god) when he performs a sudden mad action which contradicts the ordinary pattern of his behavior: thus Agamemnon explains his rashness toward Achilles in Book XIX.

ATHENA: (Pallas Athena) Daughter of Zeus (alone), goddess of wisdom, crafts, cities and the techniques of warfare. She fights loyally for the Achaeans, moved by bitter hatred for the Trojans which presumably stems from the judgment of Paris.

BRISEIS: See CHRYSEIS.

CALCHAS: Son of Thestor, chief prophet of the Acheans. His advice is detested by Agamemnon, for it was Calchas who bade Agamemnon sacrifice his daughter Iphigeneia at Aulis before the heroes departed for Troy. This incident is not related in the *Iliad*, but Agamemnon's resentment toward the soothsayer clearly alludes to the event. Calchas orders the king to give up Chryseis to her father to end the plague and wrath of Apollo.

CHRYSEIS: Daughter of Chryses, priest of Apollo, whom Agamemnon returns to her father to end the plague sent by Apollo. Agamemnon demands Achilles' prize, the woman Briseis, to compensate for his loss.

DANAANS: See ACHAEANS.

DEIPHOBUS: Son of Priam and Hecabe, brother of Hector. He is impersonated by Athena to deceive Hector in his encounter with Achilles.

DIOMEDES: Son of Tydeus, prince of Argos. He is young, brave and powerful, and is thus naturally a counterpart for Achilles. Diomedes, however, is a perfectly integrated member of the traditional society. He is pious toward the gods, respectful toward his elders and superiors, particularly his father, and loyal to Agamemnon. His sense of honor and duty accords perfectly with his role in the war, so that he avows he would remain to wage this just war if all the other kings (including Menelaus) should abandon the effort. He is disgusted with Achilles' nonconformity and breach of discipline.

DOLON: Son of Eumedes, audacious but without steadfast courage and much attached to wealth. His soft character is emphasized by the fact that he is an only son among several sisters. He is the Trojan volunteer for the night expedition (Book X) and is killed by Diomedes.

GLAUCUS: Son of Hippolochus, prince of the Lycians under Sarpedon. His code of duty and honor, his deep respect for noble lineage, make him a counterpart for Diomedes, whom he encounters without battle (Book VI) but with an exchange of pedigrees and armor, in aristocratic style.

HADES: Son of Cronus and Rhea, lord of the Underworld, the third portion of the universe, which he received by lot.

HECTOR: Hector is in many ways an antithesis to Achilles. A man devoted to wife and child, he is the thoroughly civic-minded man. He turns his heroic nature to the service of his people. His personal honor is clearly determined by his city and family. It is for them that he fights and seeks glory; it is for them that he meets death. His whole attitude is that of dedication, and yet he cannot find it in himself to mistreat Helen, although he has no respect for Paris, who lacks real *areté* and manliness and, most important, lacks a tragic awareness of what his love has cost his people. Hector, like some sacrificial figure, takes the burden of the war on himself, knowing full well that he will die, as he tells Andromache (Bk. IV). In battle, nevertheless, he displays a wild egotism and over-intense confidence in himself which makes him disregard the advice of Polydamas. But this need not be deemed a character flaw; it can be accounted for by the inner desperation Hector must feel in fighting for what he knows is a losing cause. When he dies, Troy also dies symbolically; his confrontation with Achilles symbolizing, in addition, all the irony and deceit the gods deal out to men. Hector, alone and helpless, sacrificing himself for the good of the group, becomes at that moment the most sympathetic figure in the poem.

HECABE: Chief consort of Priam, mother of Hector and queen of Troy. Her values are traditional and possessed of little substance, marked by fear and hatred of enemies, particularly Achilles.

HELEN: Here is one of the most intriguing characters in the *Iliad*. Controlled by Aphrodite, she is also a very thoughtful woman, aware that her beauty can be a curse, aware that she is a "slave" to her passions. Yet she recognizes and appreciates men who can transcend physical appetites (unlike Paris) and be truly heroic. Thus she admires her husband in his fight against Paris, realizing that as a warrior, at least, he is a superior man, a more "manly" man. She admires Hector, not only because he treats her well, but because he too is a "man" who can devote himself to wife and city. She has many good instincts and genuinely despairs at the many deaths that her behavior brought about. She never gloats or preens herself. Still, she cannot transcend her own nature. She plays out her role or destiny as a symbol of the beauty that men fight for, ironically making themselves spiritually ugly to win it.

HEPHAESTUS: Son of Zeus and Hera, the god of crafts and fire, born lame. In his battle with the river Xanthus, he represents the elemental force of battle.

HERA: Daughter of Cronos and Rhea, sister and wife of Zeus, goddess of marriage. She is cantankerous and tricky, supporting the Achaeans unreservedly and hating the Trojans implacably.

HERMES: Son of Zeus and Maia, god of roads and wayfarers and guide of the souls of the dead (psychopomp); also, with Iris, a messenger of the gods. His role as guide of Priam in Book XXIV is deliberately ambiguous.

IDAEUS: Old Herald of Priam.

THE ILIAD

IDOMENEUS: Son of Deucalion, king of the Cretans. He is an aged hero of an ancient race, but still active, whose code of duty is to remain steadfast in every battle, and thus to conquer or to die. His role is prominent at the nadir of the Achaeans' fortunes (Book XIII).

IRIS: Messenger of the Gods.

LETO: Mother of Apollo and Artemis, and accordingly on the side of the Trojans. She plays no role in the fighting, Hermes declining to engage her in battle.

MACHAON: Son of Asclepius, chief physician for the Achaeans along with his brother, Podaleirius. He is wounded in battle, where he fights bravely.

MENELAUS: Son of Atreus, king of Sparta and brother of Agamemnon. The seduction of his wife, Helen, is the cause of the Trojan war. Menelaus is the weakest and least courageous of the Achaean lords, but the fact detracts nothing frrom his nobility and authority. Agamemnon frequently worries for the safety of his younger brother, restraining him from taking risks (as in the night raid, Book X). Menelaus is sensitive about his fortitude and his role in precipitating the long conflict.

MERIONES: Squire and nephew of Idomeneus, prominent in battle and competition in Patroclus's funeral games.

NESTOR: Son of Neleus, king of Pylos. He is the oldest lord of the Argives, given to lengthy advice and speeches about his gallant youth. He is a spur to the valor of the younger heroes and leads his men in the thick of battle, but age prevents his vigorous participation in hand-to-hand combat. As a representative of an older generation, his words are heeded and respected.

ODYSSEUS: (Ulysses) Son of Laertes, king of Ithaca. He is rugged in character like his native island, of short but massive build. Odysseus became legendary as a master of guile and exemplar of patient suffering. He participates with Diomedes in the raid on the Trojan camp, chosen by Diomedes for his cleverness. Odysseus is the hero of the *Odyssey,* Homer's other major epic which has come down to us, where his resourcefulness and patient endurance of evils bring him home to Ithaca after twenty years' absence.

Odysseus is interesting in that of all the great heroes, he seems to be the one least compelled by the honor code. He is very much concerned with his survival though he can fight well and bravely. We remember that, according to the traditional account, Odysseus tried to avoid the Trojan war by feigning madness but was tricked into revealing himself when his children were threatened with death. In the war his combination of wariness and shrewdness shows itself particularly in his decision to go on the spying expedition in Book X. In some ways, Odysseus' reliance, generally speaking, on his brain rather than brawn, makes him a pre-figuration of the "modern" hero. We see these qualities more dramatically in the *Odyssey* where his questing spirit, intelligence and resourcefulness are more thoroughly tested.

PARIS: (Alexander) Son of Priam, brother of Hector. Having seduced and married Helen, wife of Menelaus, he is responsible for the war. He can be brave but is generally slack in warfare and prefers more gentle activity. He is scolded by Helen and Hector, but defends himself in the name of Aphrodite, whose deity must not be slighted. He slays Achilles after the close of the *Iliad*.

It is one of the ironic commentaries of the *Iliad* that Paris is, indeed, a favorite of the gods. This seems to be an indirect comment on the shallowness and cruelty of the gods who would prefer a man like him to, say, Hector, whom they cannot save though they would like to (Zeus particularly loves Hector but even he is powerless to avert Destiny). Paris is what today we would call a "playboy." He is an example of what the lush life of Troy before the war could do to a man in the way of "softening" him. He is not "evil," only weak and self-indulgent, without the self-awareness of his paramour, Helen. He is one of those luxury-loving men who succeed by some clever skill or deceit in bringing down better men. Paris kills Achilles by shooting at him from the Trojan walls, piercing him in the heel with an arrow. He would never meet Achilles face to face. In a heroic age, Paris is truly decadent.

PATROCLUS: Son of Menoetius of Opus, squire of Achilles. Patroclus is to be contrasted with Achilles. He is slow to anger, always kind and full of pity for his suffering comrades. He is thus torn between loyalty to Achilles and duty to the Achaean army; he dies in the armor of Achilles at the head of the Argives. Achilles slays Hector to avenge his death.

PHOENIX: Son of Amyntor, king of the Dolopes. He was the tutor of Achilles, replacing the centaur Chiron who traditionally held that position. In the *Iliad* he sometimes acts as parent to

Achilles (as in the embassy scene, Book IX), just as Patroclus's role is analogous to that of Achilles' spouse.

POLYDAMAS: Son of Panthous, wise and of good counsel. His advice is ignored by Hector, who suffers for overruling by force the counsel of a wiser man. The role of Polydamas is in part similar to that of Odysseus or Phoenix.

POSEIDON: Son of Cronus and Rhea, god of the sea and earthquakes. He rules the watery portion of the universe, and is partial to the Argives, presumably because of Laomedon's treachery (Book XXI). He generally submits to Zeus's authority because Zeus is the elder and wiser brother.

PRIAM: Son of Laomedon, aged king of Troy. His name and harem suggest an oriental figure. He is of imperious temper (Book XXIV), yet kindly and possessed of great courage, revealed by his stealthy trip to the tent of Achilles to ransom Hector's body. He is to be contrasted to Peleus, father of Achilles. His great fall from high fortune to misery has made his name proverbial for sharp reversal. After the fall of Troy, he is killed by Neoptolemus, son of Achilles.

SARPEDON: Son of Zeus, king of Lycia, a Trojan ally. He is seen, like Hector, in the context of family and nation, and is a counterpart to Hector. His death at the hands of Patroclus presages Achilles' slaying of Hector.

STHENELUS: Son of Capaneus, squire of Diomedes. He is disrespectful toward his father, asserting that he and Diomedes excel their parents (Book V); he takes umbrage at a rebuke from Agamemnon. He is thus a foil to play up the dutifulness of Diomedes.

TALTHYBIUS: Famous herald of Agamemnon, whose name has come to represent a loyal herald.

TEUCER: Bastard son of Telamon, and thus half-brother of the greater Aias. He is skilled at archery, firing from behind the great shield of Aias. When the action of the *Iliad* is completed, Telamon rejects him after the suicide of Aias.

THERSITES: A rank-and-file Achaean warrior, of common birth, a birth which is emphasized by his ugliness. (Note he is the only ugly character in the *Iliad*.) He protests against the war and is struck by Odysseus for challenging his superiors. There is an implicit comparison between Thersites and Achilles.

THETIS: Daughter of Nereus, immortal wife of the mortal Peleus and mother of Achilles. Zeus and Hephaestus are obligated to her for saving their lives when in childhood they were threatened. In the case of Zeus she supports the new ruler against the older generation (Cronus), which is parallel to her support for Achilles against Agamemnon.

XANTHUS: The river is known to mortals as Scamander, and also the god of the river. Staunch defender of Troy, he is defeated in battle by Hephaestus (the Greeks thought of flames destroying pools and rivers rather than water quenching fires).

ZEUS: Son of Cronus and Rhea, god of the upper air and highest Olympian deity, the "father of gods and men." He is all-powerful and all-wise, the dispenser of destiny, yet is often deceived by Hera. His role is thus a fusion of religious traditions. As chief figure of an essentially tribal family, he may be compared with Agamemnon. His rebellion against Cronus, however, and his mighty aloofness, link him with Achilles.

CRITICAL COMMENTARY

THE HOMERIC QUESTION. During the last past of the nineteenth century and early part of the twentieth century, the prevailing opinion among Homeric scholars was that there was no such person as Homer. It was believed that the *Iliad* and the *Odyssey* represented a patch-work of poems built around a central theme. In the case of the *Iliad*, this central theme was the anger of Achilles. It became a favorite game among these scholars to find the original Anger poem by striking out all the lines they considered to be later interpolations. Some cut the Iliad down to a sixth of its original size, proclaiming that this was the original Anger of Achilles. These analysts (as they are called) then argued about the subsequent stratification of the poem—some maintaining that the poem grew gradually, others that one poet incorporated many smaller poems into the original Anger—but they could reach no common opinion.

It was also argued that the *Odyssey*, too, was built around a central theme, the return of Odysseus, and contained many additions that were not in the original although, they agreed, the *Odyssey*, more than the *Iliad*, appears to be the work of one poet. They examined the *Iliad* from many aspects—archeological, structural, linguistic—and decided which passages were interpolated. The building of the Achaean wall (Book VII) and the embassy to Achilles (Book IX) all analysts agreed were later insertions.

It was not until the end of the first World War that the tide began to turn. Scholars, dissatisfied with the results of the dissection that had been carried out on Homer's corpus, became aware of the unity of thought in the *Iliad* and the *Odyssey*. J. A. Scott (see bibliography), Sheppard, and Drerup were the first of those to see the poem as unified. They stressed Homer's originality, even to the point of denying the existence of Troy—although Schliemann's discoveries had been known for many years. These men worked hard to prove that the *Iliad* and the *Odyssey* were written by one person, but their work suffered because of an imperfect understanding of the mechanics of oral verse-making.

Most modern criticism dates from 1928, when the first work of

Milman Parry was published (see bibliography). Now that scholars could be certain that they were dealing with the work of one poet, they could proceed without hesitation to give the *Iliad* and the *Odyssey* the analysis these poems deserve. There remains, however, a small band of classical scholars who still believe in multiple authorship for the two poems.

The most vociferous of these critics is Denys L. Page, who, in his two books (see bibliography), has applied to the *Iliad* and the *Odyssey* a logic so overwhelming that it obscures any poetry that may be present. In Chapter I, for example, of the Appendix to his *History and the Homeric Iliad*, Professor Page analyzes the episode of the embassy to Achilles. He concludes that Phoenix was not in the original version, but was inserted into the embassy episode, which in turn was inserted into the original *Iliad*. He never asks why a later poet would insert the character of Phoenix, and consequently he fails to see Phoenix's importance in introducing a new sense of morality into the *Iliad*—a morality that Achilles accepts *and acts upon* in the remainder of the poem.

Porter, S. T.

CONCLUSION

We shall give below, now, some hints and motifs in the *Iliad* which, hopefully, will deepen the student's appreciation, without presuming to offer anything like a "complete" or systematic interpretation. The authors are indebted to Professor Howard N. Porter, whose insights into Homer form the basis of their understanding, both of the work and, in large part, of themselves.

THE ROLE OF THE GODS IN *THE ILIAD*. But, on the whole, critics accepted the integrity of the two poems, and with the aid of psychology, anthropology, and the techniques of the new critics, produced perceptive analyses. E. R. Dodds, for example, in chapter I of *The Greeks and the Irrational,* gave a modern interpretation of the role of the gods in Homer. To the earlier critics, the gods were merely comic figures who interfered in the affairs of mortals whenever they could. The poem, they said, suffered, since human beings were not free to work out their own destinies: there is scarcely a fight or council that is not influenced by one god or another.

By carefully examining all the examples of divine intervention, Professor Dodds concluded that the gods were used by Homer to explain extraordinary events and actions. Thus, when a warrior shoots an arrow farther that usual, the warrior will say that Ares, the god of war, helped him to pull back the bowstring. There is no other explanation for having shot so well. The gods were used to explain bad actions, as well as good ones; for example, in Book XIX of the *Iliad,* Agamemnon blames not himself for his argument with Achilles, but Zeus and the Erinys. It was by means of the gods that the characters in Homer's poems believed that they could explain all acts that were not rational, that is, that were not the normal actions of a normal mortal. Anything out of the ordinary must, they reasoned, be the results of a god's machination.

Homer, the poet behind the characters, had the power to make these gods appear. Thus, if a character interpreted the flight of an eagle to be a propitious sign from Zeus, Homer can, and usually does, show us Zeus sending forth the eagle. It is but a short step beyond such action to have gods visible to us, the audience, and not visible to the characters they will be affecting, for instance, in any one of the councils of the gods of Olympus.

Odysseus, the craftiest of mortals, both in the *Iliad* and the *Odyssey*, constantly has Athena, the goddess of craft, by his side, aiding him whenever she can. But her presence does not detract from Odysseus' stature. In fact, it enhances his stature, for what Athena's presence states is that Odysseus's powers are so far beyond ordinary mortals', that they can be explained only in terms of divine help —great praise, indeed! Athena is the natural choice for Odysseus' divine champion, for she is the ageless personification of all Odysseus' talents.

But the Greek gods are not merely literary devices that explain unusual attributes and occurrences. They have personalities as well developed as any of Homer's human characters. They even fight among themselves.

Observe that the gods—and only the gods—are *comic* in the *Iliad*. They have not the dignity of Homer's mortal figures, for they cannot suffer or die.

DIGRESSIONS: There is another aspect of Homer's technique that should be examined—his habit of interrupting the flow of the narrative with a digression that, having little to do with the point in question, tends to retard the action. A modern reader who expects to proceed uninterrupted may find the technique disconcerting. The modern reader does not expect to find, for example, a battle scene in which, in addition to the fighting itself, so much attention is spent on the genealogies of minor characters. Authors after Homer were careful to "set the scene" by mentioning the characters beforehand, so that in a tense scene they were not obliged to introduce new characters for the first time. But these later authors were writing their works. They had time, before the work was read, to rearrange their scenes, so that everything seemed "natural."

Homer, on the other hand, was not working with the written page, but with the spoken word. He could not erase or rearrange what he had spoken. This does not mean that the poem proceeded without plan or that there was no unity to the whole work; what it does imply is that, as Homer recited, certain words would trigger other associated words, which he would then present in a digression, always making sure to return to his starting point.

Not only men but also inanimate objects received this treatment. A bow, for example, brought into battle might be given a history

THE ILIAD

as complete as any warrior's, being traced back in some instances to the god Hephaestus. Just as Homer increases the stature of a warrior who has a minor role by endowing him with noble ancestors, so does he increase the stature of a bow (or any other weapon) which is about to slay or wound a mighty warrior. Such a bow is the bow of Pandarus, which, before it sends an arrow to wound Menelaus, receives a full genealogy (Book IV). The fact that this commentary on the soldier or object lessens the tension was no objection to Homer, for tension and suspense played small parts in his story-telling technique, since his audience was fully familiar with the story.

But, like Homer's use of the gods, this technique of stress through digression never became a mechanical device. If it did, every important object would come complete with genealogy, and such is not the case. Erich Auerbach, in chapter I of his *Mimesis* (see bibliography), discusses Homer's use of digression and compares it with the terse style of the Old Testament. He maintains that Homer describes so many objects as fully as he does because of a need to externalize everything, that is, to present everything in full perspective. But Auerbach's theory can not be the full answer, for obviously Homer can not externalize all objects that he mentions —only some of them.

SENIORITY AND AUTHORITY. The respect due seniority and rank is a pervasive theme in the *Iliad*. Achilles rejects traditional values, personified by Diomedes, which would bind him in loyalty to one endowed with greater authority by the sole virtue of his status. Confident in his youth and valor, he challenges Agamemnon's supremacy and is even moved to slay him. He is restrained only by a whisper of conscience or a deity. In the funeral games for Patroclus, under the serene arbitration of Achilles, Homer presents us with an alternative version of the quarrel. In the chariot race, Antilochus, with youthful rashness, cuts off Menelaus, and thus does offense to the superior king's honor. Antilochus, however, yields modestly to Menelaus's authority, and Menelaus, for his part, relents and does not abuse his rank. We may also note that Poseidon yields before his brother Zeus, who is older and wiser, without active defiance.

RANSOM AND COMPROMISE. The *Iliad* opens with an unsuccessful effort at ransom. Chryses, the priest of Apollo, offers "innumerable gifts" to Agamemnon for the return of his daughter, Chryseis, but the king refuses to accept the exchange and casts out the priest with threats. In the embassy to Achilles (Book IX), Agamemnon again offers "innumerable gifts" to induce Achilles to return to battle, but Achilles is adamant. At the end of the poem, however, Achilles breaks his vow to the spirit of Patroclus, delivers the corpse to Priam in return for "innumerable gifts," that he will throw the body of Hector to the dogs to feed on, and which he describes as a "worthy" ransom. Achilles has learned that for mortals there are no absolutes, that men must relent before a proper recompense; thus life is the interplay between natural or social forces and subjective passions and principles, where compromise cannot be avoided.

CODES AND CHARACTERS. In the *Iliad* characters are more than personalities. They are frequently seen as representatives of social codes, whose relations with one another in the context of the action serve as experiments in modes of behavior. Thus we may see Diomedes as the representative of the prevailing traditions among the Achaeans. His sense of duty, piety, loyalty and respect accords perfectly with his social role. Achilles, the nonconformist, breaks the code in the spirit of innerdirected individualism. Idomeneus, on the other hand, represents an almost total immersion in the social environment, which, in the context of his advanced age and the archaic society over which he rules, may be considered the older form. Patroclus, by virtue of his position as squire of Achilles, is perhaps characterized by an ideal blend of individualism and social duty, which emerges as profound kindness. He "dwells, in a peculiar way, at the very center of the poem" (Simone Weil).

SIMILES. The similes in the *Iliad* are not arbitrary. It may be assumed that they invariably illustrate or expand the meaning of the passage and of the poem. Note that in Book I, when Chryses addresses his prayer to Apollo, asking that the god may win back his daughter Chryseis, his invocation begins with the epithet, "lord of the silver bow." Our attention is thus directed to the god's function as dispenser of death by disease, which becomes prominent immediately following. A few lines further down (1. 47), the god Apollo descends like night. Night and darkness are commonly associated with death, which motivates this simile. These examples are illustrative of how the student should approach the Homeric rhetoric. For the role of natural metaphors, which expresses the elemental force of warfare, see the COMMENTARY on pages 89-90 in Book XIV of the resume of the text.

SUMMATION. No great work is reducible, in the final analysis, to a few "points." If a work is great, it in some ways defies precise summation. It projects a sense of the mystery of existence and of the comedy and tragedy of life. What the student can best do, therefore, is not to seek for a definitive meaning to the poem, because there is none, but, rather, to approach the work from a point of view that may interest him. For example, let us say that it is the problem of war, itself, that interests him. From this point of view, the *Iliad* provides a magnificent treatment of the overall tragedy of war, its effects on the innocent, on rich and poor alike, the warrior and the worker. It reveals the stresses and strains that complicate action, turning men into beasts and then making finer men out of them again, as with Achilles. War, in the *Iliad,* is the testing ground for men's souls, a crucible which tests every aspect of a man's makeup. Note how the various crises expose the weaknesses of Agamemnon and Menelaus, the sponsors of the siege, the strengths of Diomedes and Odysseus. The multi-faceted personality of Odysseus, in particular, is tested in all its aspects by the changing requirements of war. We see him protecting himself when he can, being brave when that is warranted, employing his oratory when that, too, is needed. We see cowards and brave men, and sometimes men inextricably doomed, try as they might to save themselves, as in the case of Lycaon in Book XXI. We see the effect of war upon love and *vice versa,* in the case of Paris and Helen. We see the tragically doomed yet happily married family of Hector and Andromache. We see how friends, parents, and lovers react to the fact of death. And, finally, the sensitive reader will just feel the power, horror and grandeur of war, itself, as an aspect of existence, of the eternal *Eris.*

THE PROBLEM OF WAR. War is, after all, man's greatest social problem, and the *Iliad* suggests some of the reasons for this. For, if men behave magnificently in war, the causes of war are, generally, inglorious. There is the suggestion, indeed, that no cause for war can be truly glorious. The bravery of the men at war always transcends their reasons for having to be brave. Consider the Paris-Helen affair and what results from it. Though one can argue that the war supports the value of marriage customs, no one denies that a war of ten years duration is tragically too long for any social affront. But once the blood lust begins, the need for glory and loot grow with it, and the original cause for the war fades into the background. Remember how eagerly the Greeks rush to their ships when Agamemnon fools them and tells them that they can go home. It is a great tragi-comic moment and shows how easily our ideals can be punctured under the stress of reality.

Does the *Iliad* suggest a solution to war? Perhaps, but only by implication. Certainly the behavior of Paris and Helen, of Achilles and Agamemnon is criticized. And the one thing they all have in common is that they are "slaves of passion." They behave in excess of a socially determined norm. Indeed, the whole of the *Iliad* is a picture of excess, an excess of death, pride, honor, wrath, love and hate. The characters are drawn larger than life and even the rivers rise up choked to excess with dead bodies. Even the shield of Achilles fits the pattern; it is the supreme shield, the ultimate of shields for the ultimate of men. Yet, ironically, it contains the only picture of balance and harmony in the *Iliad*. Perhaps, then, an avoidance of rash or excessive behavior is one approach to solving the problem of war. The Daughters of Zeus must be respected or *Até* triumphs. It is as simple—and complex—as that.

THE QUESTION OF DEATH. As important is the question of death, itself. It is not only that the *Iliad* gives vivid and interesting pictures of death and of man's relationship to it, though it certainly does do this. The significance of this subject is, rather, that the *Iliad* poses the entire question of the *value* of death in relation to the *value* of life. Since death, Homer seems to be saying, is a constant presence in life, we may the better see how men value their lives—life itself as a quality of existence—when they are close to that presence. Values are put forward with which to counter death: honor, glory, sex, wealth. But, as with Achilles, we learn that they will never do. Life must become its own value if death is to lose its horror and fear for us. If it does, life will not be poisoned, and the inevitable can be accepted without distorting our lives and societies with the creation of honor codes in order to achieve a sense of glory and a fleeting remembrance in man's memory.

GODS AND MAN. Another, and final, point of view from which to see the *Iliad* is the question of the gods. Longinus, an ancient Greek critic, wrote that "Homer changed gods into men and men into gods." Indeed, this is what happens. The gods lack tragic stature, however, only because they do not operate in time, as man does. Only man, in his very mortality, can suffer and, therefore, only man need search for meaning so as to reconcile himself to the suffering, the vanity of existence. Homer appears to be saying that, although the gods are more powerful than man, in the final analysis, they are *only* forces, in a sense, inanimate. They have meaning only in relation to man, himself. Man can learn morally to take up a humble, balanced attitude toward such forces, as Achilles does learn. But it is man who learns, not the forces. Remember how badly Aphrodite and Ares, the two malicious causes or forces in nature, and, especially, in their relation to this war, are treated by Homer. He shows Aphrodite wounded by Diomedes, and Ares mocked by men and gods alike. Man, however, has his own inherent dignity by virtue of being mortal, and it is the stature of tragic man that Homer finally affirms.

SAMPLE EXAMINATION
QUESTIONS AND ANSWERS

QUESTION 1: What is the estimated date of the Trojan War?

ANSWER: The Greeks of the Classical Period had many guesses concerning the date of the Trojan War. These guesses ranged in date from 1334 to 1150 B.C., the standard date being 1184, which was the estimate of Eratosthenes, a Greek of the third century B.C. who compiled a chronology of major events in Greek history. Later scholars had no other evidence on which to base a guess, until archeologists, digging up the ruins of Troy, discovered that one of the many towns built on this site (it is now called by the Turkish name of Hisarlik) was destroyed by fire. In addition a few corpses were found who had died through violent means, and large storage jugs were discovered in many of the houses, indicating that the city had been undergoing a prolonged siege. This city, then, was most probably the Troy of the Trojan War. From other evidence, it seems likely that the fire occurred about the year 1250, a date which coincides with the estimate of Herodotus, a Greek historian of the fifth century B.C.

QUESTION 2: What was the social structure of the Homeric Age?

ANSWER: Agamemnon, Achilles, and the other warriors of the *Iliad* are representatives of a society that was prevalent throughout the Greek-speaking world between the years 1550 and 1150 B.C. This society was similar to the society of the Middle Ages in Europe. That is, it was feudal. Life revolved around the household. Here, the master of the house presided over his household, which consisted of slaves, servants, and family. Originally, the word "family" meant the entire household, and not only relatives; the Latin phrase *pater familias*, "father of the family," really means "father of the household." The slaves were usually female, since the greatest source of slaves was from conquered cities, and it was the practice among the Greeks to slaughter all the men in any city they might capture. (The supply of mistresses for the Greeks fighting in Troy came from this same source.) Each household was surrounded by enough land to keep itself self-sufficient. There were, however, a few services that were required from outside the household: the specialized jobs of carpenters, physicians, minstrels, prophets, etc.

The householder was the nobleman of his day. The only person superior to him was the king of his land, who was, of course, also a householder. The king had the authority to call the nobles together for an assembly, where he would hear their views on the subject at hand before making the final decision.

On the battlefield far from home, the same hierarchy was maintained: the warriors were nobles, and the generals were all kings. The question of why Agamemnon was chosen to lead all the forces has not yet been satisfactorily answered. He might have been chosen solely because he was the elder brother of Menelaus, the injured party in the action that led to the Trojan War. But he was also the king of Mycenae, the most powerful Greek city of that time and, therefore, may have been considered the natural leader because of his great wealth or power (or both). He held assemblies of kings by the ships, just as kings at home were accustomed to hold assemblies of nobles.

QUESTION 3: How have scholars been able to set a date for the composition of the *Iliad*?

ANSWER: Since the *Iliad* was in origin an oral epic, that is, a poem to be recited from memory, and since it has been established that the ability to recite and compose poems of such length can exist only in an illiterate society, it is easy to see that it must have been written down soon after the introduction of writing into Greece. Through the study of inscriptions on stone and bronze (the earliest examples of the Greek alphabet still extant), it has been determined that 750 B.C. represents a likely date for the introduction of writing.

The assumption that we have a text of the *Iliad* that is at least close to the *Iliad* that Homer composed demands either that Homer himself put it on paper (or, what is more likely, dictated it to a scribe), or that the poem was handed down orally intact by a group of bards (Homeridae) until they had access to writing. This latter alternative, though possible, probably would not have kept the poem "pure" for a very long period of time. Until more facts are available, the year 750 B.C. remains a good estimate for the composition of the *Iliad*.

QUESTION 4: Describe the character of Aias, son of Oileus.

ANSWER: Aias is brave but insolent. His hot temper erupts against Idomeneus as they watch the chariot race when Idomeneus observes that Diomedes has taken the lead over Eumelus, who is Aias' favorite. Achilles stills the dissension. In the footrace he is made to slip in dung, and thus he loses to Odysseus. When he escapes a storm on his voyage home from Troy, his boastful blasphemy enrages Poseidon, who drowns him in the sea.

QUESTION 5: Why do Athena and Hera rage so implacably against the Trojans and their allies?

ANSWER: In the background of the poem lies the famous judgment of Paris. Hera, Athena and Aphrodite consulted Paris to determine which of the three was most beautiful. Each, moreover, offered a reward consistent with her powers, should she be selected. Paris rejected Hera's offer of power and Athena's gift of prowess, to accept the hand of Helen by virtue of Aphrodite's good offices. The spurned goddesses retaliate with divine fury.

QUESTION 6: How do the characters of deities contrast with the characters of mortals in the *Iliad*?

ANSWER: It has been said that only the gods are comic in the *Iliad*, because they cannot suffer or die. Thus note the unquenchable laughter of the gods when Hephaestus lamely bustles in their service (Book I) and compare the humorous tale of Aphrodite's infidelity with Ares, in Book VIII of the *Odyssey*.

The gods of Homer have long offended moralists by their naughty behavior. They are in fact endowed with all the worst vices of human society. Xenophanes, an ancient Greek philosophical poet who was born in 565 B.C. and thus lived in all likelihood within two centuries of Homer, inscribed the following critique:

> Homer and Hesiod attributed all things to the gods,
> Whatever is reproachful and blameworthy among human beings,
> Stealing and adultery and deceiving one another.

On the other hand, the gods may be awesome and austere, like Zeus when he nods and the heavens quake, or Aphrodite when she rouses the passion of love in Paris and Helen (Book III).

QUESTION 7: What are patronymics?

ANSWER: Citizens in ancient Greece, who had only one proper name, were frequently identified by the father's name. Thus the two Aiantes (plural of Aias) are distinguished by reference to their fathers, Telamon and Oileus. Rather than include the phrase "son of," standard forms, called patronymics, were in use, which were applied to the son but indicated the name of the father. Thus

Peleides, or "son of Peleus," is Achilles, Atreides, "son of Atreus," is either Agamemnon or Menelaus, while the two may be referred to by the plural form, Atreidae. Tydeides, "son of Tydeus," is of course Diomedes. Telamoniades is the patronymic of Telamonian Aias, who is also identified by the adjectival form of his father's name, Telamonius. The reader can easily see to whom the following patronymics may refer. Oiliades, Priamides, Menoetiades, Neliades, Nestorides. To avoid confusion, we have generally avoided patronymics in the text of this book.

QUESTION 8: Was Homer blind?

ANSWER: Among the many legends that developed concerning Homer's life was the story that he was a blind poet. It might be expected that a blind person would tend to become a bard, since not only was there little else he could do to earn a living, but his sense of hearing and rhythm might be more developed than that of a person with sight.

The legend of Homer's blindness gained impetus from the mention by Homer of Demodocus, a blind poet in the Phaeacian court (*Odyssey*, Book VIII). In addition, in the famous Hymn to Apollo, at one time attributed to Homer (see INTRODUCTION), the poet speaks in the first person and mentions that he is blind man, living in Chios. About Homer, however, the strongest biographical statement that can be made with any degree of certitude is that he was an Ionian (Chios, we may add, is in Ionia.)

QUESTION 9: What are Homeric epithets?

ANSWER: The oral style of composition demands units or building blocks larger than the single word, if the poet is to recite without pause; thus phrases and whole lines and passages are at the poet's command, which he works with to produce his poem (see INTRODUCTION, pp. 1-19). Among the most common types of poetic formulas is the personal adjective (or adjectives), called epithets, which are frequently or always associated with the name of a particular character. Thus the epithets which describe Achilles may be *dios*: "divine;" *Podas okus*: "swift-footed;" *podarkes dios*: "quick-footed divine." Epithets associated with Odysses are *polymetis*: "adventurous;" *polytlas dios*: "much-suffering divine." Epithets of Menelaus are *boen agathos*: "good at the cry;" *areiphilos*: "dear to Ares;" *anthus*: "tawny" or "tawny-haired;" and *areios*: "warlike." The following entire line is a formulaic description of Agamemnon. The parts following the parentheses may be used alone as shorter formulas: *heros Atreides euru (kreion Agamemnon*: "the hero (son of Atreus wide-ruling Agamemnon)". Also he

THE ILIAD

is referred to as *anax andron*: 'lord of men;" and *poimeni laon* (dative): "shepherd of the people."

Zeus has a host of epithets, among which are *metieta*: "counselling;" *aigiochoio*: "aegis-holding;" *hypsibremetes*: "high-thundering;" *terpipikeraunoi* (dative): "rejoicing in lightning;" *nephelegereta*: "cloud-gathering;" *hypermenei*: "of great strength."

QUESTION 10: What is the definition of *"areté"* and its function in the poem?

ANSWER: *"Areté"* is defined as excellence or a power of excellence. It is what each hero strove to achieve, the quality which gave him distinction in the honor code society of Homeric Greece.

QUESTION 11: What are three structural patterns of the *Iliad*?

ANSWER: First, there is the individual story of Achilles, of his "wrath" (mentioned importantly in the opening lines of the poem) and of his tragic destiny. Secondly, there is the story of a portion of the Trojan War (though the beginning and the end of the war are suggested by various means), a microcosm of the nature of all wars. Thirdly, there is a dramatization of the relationship between men and the gods, an attempt to portray man's relationship to the forces of nature and of the cosmos outside of himself.

QUESTION 12: How does Homer unify these three patterns?

ANSWER: These patterns are linked together by means of a number of key themes such as death, honor, war, and the philosophical theme of *Eris*. Thus honor, for example, is a pervasive theme which defines both the conduct of Achilles and the terms under which the war, itself, is fought (remember the meeting of Diomedes and Glaucus, the fight over the dead bodies of the heroes Patroclus and Sarpedon, *etc.*). It is, indeed, over a point of honor—Menelaus' honor—that the very war is being fought. Finally, the honor theme affects the relationship of the gods to men, though it is not a mutual relationship. While men must honor the gods, these immortal powers need not behave honorably towards men. The gods play favorites within the limits determined by destiny, striving to protect their own rather than to preserve the right. If comedy is made out of the marital troubles of Zeus, tragedy ensues from the dishonorable behavior of the gods toward men, their receptions and betrayals of trust.

QUESTION 13: W. B. Yeats has asked: "What theme had Homer but Original Sin." In what sense is this true?

ANSWER: Original Sin, the disobedience of Adam and Eve in the *Bible*, can, by extension, be seen to imply some basic or innate defect in man which brings about his suffering. In both the *Bible* and the *Iliad*, this moral defect is Pride, a flaw which allows one's passions to overcome his reason. And, just as the pride of Adam and Eve leads them into a sin which, according to the *Bible*, affects everyone, so the pride of Achilles leads him into actions which, in the context of the *Iliad*, affect all. In both cases, moreover, this "sin" of pride is archetypal (the Trojan War, in the *Iliad*, being a microcosm for the world and Achilles its Everyman). As Achilles is presented as having the greatest *areté* of any hero in the *Iliad*, it would appear that the greater the *areté*, the greater the potentiality for pride. But if Achilles represents a tragic extreme, he also reflects the qualities which, to greater or lesser degrees, exist in all men and lead to their suffering. Insofar as Homer uses the theme of pride as a central concern and this moral defect is implicit in the concept of "original sin," it may, then, be said that the *Iliad* does deal significantly with what we, today, might call "original sin."

QUESTION 14: What is Homer's attitude towards war?

ANSWER: Homer's attitude is ambiguous. He says that wars are "horrible" and that the Trojan War, in particular, contained many horrors. His descriptions of death, gory in detail, further imply a horror and detestation of war. Yet, when the armies line up with their plumes and spears and shining armor, he says that it is a magnificent sight.

QUESTION 15: How many different kinds of love relationships does the *Iliad* portray?

ANSWER: A variety of love relationships is portrayed. There is the love between friends, that of Achilles of Patroclus, the married love of Hector and Andromache, the erotic love of Paris and Helen, the parental love of Thetis towards Achilles and of Priam and Hecabe towards Hector, and, finally, the love different gods display to their favorite heroes in saving them from disaster (*e.g.*, Aphrodite's saving of Paris from Menelaus). All these love relationships further extend the range of human experience presented in the *Iliad*.

QUESTION 16: What role does nature play in the poem?

ANSWER: For the most part, nature is used merely as a dynamic backdrop to the war. There are, however, two important special uses of nature in the work. First, Homer draws many of his similes from images of nature such as the sea, storms, lion attacks, waving fields of grain, mountains, *etc.* Secondly, Homer personifies the River Xanthus, in Book XXI, making it complain of Achilles' murderous rampage.

QUESTION 17: What hero wounds what goddess in battle? What is the incident's significance?

ANSWER: Diomedes wounds Aphrodite in Book V. The event glorifies man at the expense of the gods and may, in particular, be seen as a condemnation of Aphrodite, whose influence helped to start the war.

QUESTION 18: What god is the butt of jokes from the other gods and why?

ANSWER: Hephaestus is mocked by the other gods because he is lame, there being little of the compassion for cripples in that heroic age that we have today. Another reason for this mockery may be that Hephaestus, though an artist, works with his hands, an occupation which, to the aristocratic gods, places him socially beneath them.

QUESTION 19: What figure does Homer describe in great detail who is not an aristocrat?

ANSWER: Thersites is a commoner whom Odysseus beats because he dared to speak out sensibly against continuing the war. He is described as being physically ugly.

QUESTION 20: What personification of what force is used by both Achilles and Agamemnon to explain their rash behavior?

ANSWER: *Até*, the goddess of Folly, Ruin, or Impulse, is so used.

QUESTION 21: What symbol does Homer use to demonstrate the inexorability of Fate?

ANSWER: A huge pair of scales is held aloft by Zeus who places the destinies of Troy and the Achaeans in the two measures. The scale dips down on the Trojan side, dooming them. This shows that even Zeus cannot change the course of destined events, however much he may sympathize with the Trojans. Instead, all he can do is to give the Trojans momentary success which, ironically, kills more of them in the end than if he had allowed the battle to take its natural course.

BIBLIOGRAPHY

TRANSLATIONS OF *THE ILIAD*.

CHASE, ALSTON HURD, AND WILLIAM G. PERRY, JR. New York: Bantam Books, 1960 (pb*).

LANG, ANDREW, WALTER LEAF, AND ERNEST MYERS. New York: Modern Library, (also in pb).

LATTIMORE, RICHMOND. Chicago: University of Chicago Press, 1961 (pb).

POPE, ALEXANDER. Oxford, England: The Oxford University Press, 1951.

RIEU, E. V. Harmondsworth, England: Penguin Books, 1961 (pb).

ROUSE, W. H. D. New York: The New American Library, 1954 (pb).

EVELYN-WHITE, HUGH G. *Hesiod, The Homeric Hymns, and Homerica*. ("Loeb Classical Library Series.") Cambridge, Mass.: Harvard University Press, 1959.

GENERAL

ALLEN, T. W. *Homer: The Origins and Transmissions*. Oxford: The Oxford University Press, 1924.

ARNOLD, MATTHEW. *On Translating Homer*. London: Routledge, 1905.

AUERBACH, ERICH. *Mimesis*. Princeton, N. J.: The Princeton University Press, 1953 (also in pb). (See especially Chapter 1, "Odysseus' Scar," reprinted in *Homer*, ed. by Steiner; see below.)

BASSET, S. E. *The Poetry of Homer*. Berkeley: The University of California Press, 1938.

BESPALOFF, RACHEL. *On the Iliad*. New York: Pantheon Books, 1947 (also in pb).

BLEGEN, CARL W. *Troy*. Cambridge, England: The Cambridge University Press, 1961 (pb).

*(pb) means paperback

BOWRA, C. M. *Tradition and Design in the Iliad*. Oxford: The Oxford University Press, 1950.

CARPENTER, RHYS. *Folk tale, Saga, and Fiction in the Homeric Epics*. Berkeley: The University of California Press, 1946 (also in pb).

CHADWICK, JOHN. *The Decipherment of Linear B*. Harmondsworth, England: Penguin Books, 1961 (pb).

DODDS, E. R. *The Greeks and the Irrational*. Berkeley: The University of California Press, 1963 (pb).

FINLEY, M. I. *The World of Odysseus*. New York: Meridian Books, 1959 (pb).

JAEGER, WERNER. Volume I of *Paideia: The Ideals of Greek Culture*. Oxford: Basil Blackwell, 1954. (See especially pp. 3-57.)

JEBB, R. C. *Homer: An Introduction*. Glasgow: J. Macelhose and Son, 1905.

KIRK, G. S. *The Songs of Homer*. Cambridge: The Cambridge University Press, 1962.

LEVY, B. R. *The Sword from the Rock*. London: 1953.

LORIMER, H. L. *Homer and the Monuments*. London: Macmillan & Co., 1950.

LORD, ALBERT B. *The Singer of Tales*. Cambridge, Mass.: The Harvard University Press, 1960.

MURRAY, GILBERT. *The Rise of the Greek Epic*. Oxford: The Oxford University Press, 1960 (pb).

MYRES, J. L. *Homer and his Critics*. London: Routledge and Kegan Paul, 1958.

NILSSON, MARTIN. *Homer and Mycenae*. London: Methuen and Co., 1933.

O'NEILL, EUGENE, JR. "The Localization of Metrical Wordtypes in the Greek Hexameter," *Yale Classical Studies*, VIII (1942).

PAGE, DENYS L. *History and the Homeric Iliad.* Berkeley: University of California Press, 1963 (pb).

——————. *The Homeric Odyssey.* Oxford: The Oxford University Press, 1955.

PARRY, MILMAN. "L'epithète traditionelle chez Homère," Paris: Les Belles Lettres, 1928.

——————. "Studies in Epic Technique and Verse-making," *Harvard Studies in Classical Philology*, XLI (1929); XLIII (1932).

PLATNAUER, MAURICE (ed.). *Fifty Years of Classical Scholarship.* Oxford: Basil Blackwell, 1954. (See especially pp. 1-38.)

PORTER, HOWARD N. "The Early Greek Hexameter," *Yale Classical Studies,* XII (1951).

SCOTT, JOHN A. *The Unity of Homer.* Berkeley: The University of California Press, 1921.

SHEPPARD, J. T. *The Pattern of the Iliad.* London: Methuen & Co., 1922.

SNELL, BRUNO. *The Discovery of the Mind.* Cambridge, Mass.: The Harvard University Press, 1953. (See especially Chapter 1.)

——————. *Poetry and Society: The Role of Poetry in Ancient Greece.* Indiana University Press, 1961.

STEINER, GEORGE, AND ROBERT FAGLES (eds.). *Homer: A Collection of Critical Essays.* Englewood Cliffs, N. J.: Prentice-Hall, 1962 (pb).

WACE, ALAN J. B., AND FRANK H. STUBBINGS. *A Companion to Homer.* London: Macmillan & Co., 1962.

WADE-GERY, H. T. *The Poet of the Iliad.* Cambridge: The Cambridge University Press, 1952.

WEIL, SIMONE. *The Iliad or The Poem of Force.* Wallingford, Pa.: Pendle Hill, 1957 (pb).

WHITMAN, C. *Homer and the Heroic Tradition.* Cambridge, Mass.: The Harvard University Press, 1959.